TITLE & COVER:

RED:

The element of fire.
Purifies, protects, brings light, gives life.
Strength, vitality, abundance.
Connection to earth, grounding, manifestation.

TRIANGLE:

Spirituality, rise, uplift, ascension, evolution.
The three primary spiritual qualities,
which man is called to discover
and develop in his/her life:
Love-Wisdom-Power.

ESOTERIC ANSWERS

THE
RED
BOOK

Esoteric Teachings,
Meditations,
and Healing Directions
for All Vital Questions

GEORGIOS MYLONAS
GEOM!*

Important Note
The recommendations made in this book should not be considered a replacement for formal medical or mental treatment. A physician should be consulted in all matters relating to health, including any symptoms that require medical attention. Anyone who has emotional, mental, or physical problems should seek professional consultation before attempting any of these practices. While the information and the suggestions in this book are believed to be safe and accurate, the author cannot accept liability for any harm as a result of the use or misuse of these practices. This book is intended as general information and for educational purposes.

First English edition 2021
© Georgios Mylonas
All rights reserved.

Georgios Mylonas (Geom!*)
Teacher and author on methods of energy healing, personal development and spiritual advancement
The School of Reiki, Athens
www.energiesoflight.com
www.universityofreiki.com
www.reikiathens.com
e-mail: reiki@reiki.gr

Edited by Christiana Kanaki
www.christianakanaki.com

ISBN: 9798462061943

Ten percent of the proceeds from this book go to charity.

CONTENTS

INTRODUCTION

———————— ❋ ————————

Over the last years, due to my healing and spiritual work and occupation, I have received a large number of questions and requests for answers and guidance, for help and healing, through the energy and spiritual methods I study, practice, and teach: self-knowledge and self-improvement, reiki and energy healing, introspection and meditation, esoteric philosophy and metaphysics.

In this project, I have gathered some answers, guidance, and directions to share with you, as I believe they will help a greater number of people.

They cover all topics: relationships and family, abundance and work, emotions and health, personal growth and development, the meaning and purpose of life, overcoming anxiety, stress, fear, anger, and sadness, all the problems and challenges of life, and also existential, spiritual, esoteric, and metaphysical issues.

All texts are personal thoughts and opinions and do not pontificate on the subject in any way. The reader should be completely free to think and judge if they inspire him/her, if they express him/her, if they help him/her, and to what extent. One can keep whatever one wants. What is written in this book is not THE Absolute Truth on any given subject, just a view of the Truth – my own view, according to what I have learned but also what I have personally experienced.

These texts, which include answers to many questions, as well as meditations, exercises, and energy healing techniques, were compiled and made into two books, which can be read independently or one after the other. Some topics and questions are repeated in the two books, but the answers are worded differently each time, something that will help readers to better understand and internalize these simple but oh-so-vital ideas. The reader can start from either of the two books he/she wishes or read only the texts/topics that interest him/her from both books.

The books are entitled "Esoteric Answers: The Red Book" and "Esoteric Answers 2: The Blue Book."

Moreover, this is not a simple reading but an energetic one. It will elevate you, it will strengthen you, it will fill you with positivity, light, and joy. Feel it, observe it, and enjoy it, as much as possible! You will receive inspiration and guidance for all areas of your life.

The answers, the meditations, and all the texts have been written with the intention of your highest good, the highest good of all. They have been empowered, attuned to energies of health, vitality, abundance, prosperity, bliss, serenity, freedom, and completeness – the brightest energies of the greatest enlightenment. Open your mind and heart and receive them!

From the depths of my heart, I wish this work inspires, helps, elevates, illuminates, and enlightens as many people as possible, to the greatest degree possible!

For the Highest Good, the Highest Good of All.

With Love,
Infinite Love!

Georgios Mylonas (Geom!*)

ABUNDANCE AND RELATIONSHIPS

❋

The two most frequently asked questions in the world and a (first) answer!

> *How can I have more abundance in my life? How can I not have to push myself financially so much, and have a little more ease and time for the important things?*
>
> *How can I create a beautiful romantic-love relationship, which will be good and positive?*

You want abundance and prosperity. You want beautiful, nice, positive relationships, absolute love, and heavenly romance. You're doing the right thing! You deserve them to the fullest and more than that. But have you decided about them? Have you chosen them? Really, and how much? At

1

what percentage? Superficially and confusingly or deeply and clearly? Partially or totally? Consciously or drowsily and lethargically?

Choice and decision. Two words, two concepts that are very important spiritually. Two words and concepts for deeper thinking and contemplation, for introspection and meditation. People desire different things. They desire them a little indifferently, though. Without tension, without passion. The impulse, the driving force, and the energy are missing. Almost always, those who do not have, those who are not, and those who do not experience something they desire, have not made a decision. They have not decided actively to experience it, to have it or to become it. They have not chosen it. They have not decided it truly, totally, intensely, deeply, completely, and consciously and they have not chosen it the same way – truly, totally, intensely, deeply, completely, and consciously.

To become something you want to be, to have something you want to have and to experience something that you want to experience, you need to decide it. To choose it. From within you, from deep within you. From your core, from your center, and with all your being. With body, mind, spirit, and soul, with your energy and will. All your being should want and consciously choose it, decide it and move toward it.

People desire abundance. But they do not experience it, not to the extent that they desire. They do not choose it, they do not decide it, they do not move toward it. People desire love, romance, and good relationships, but they do not decide about them, they do not choose them, they do not move toward them. The human ego prefers a tepid, fluid uncertainty, something that is familiar to it and gives it a relative sense of security, even though it is completely fake and notional. Pain, sadness, fear, and negativity, in all their forms, are addictive substances. Remember this.

On the other hand, our spirit, our true inner self, knows that its nature is abundance. It is abundance and it wants to experience abundance on the material level as well. It knows that its nature is love, romance, and well-connected relationships, and it wants to experience them in the outside world as well. So, there is a force outward, upward, and forward. And another one downward, backward, toward the known and the same. Which one will win? Each person decides and chooses individually and personally. Every single moment, as well as in the course of life as a whole.

If you desire abundance, greater prosperity, and ease in your life, decide and choose it. Blatantly. Consciously. Totally. Truly. Intensely and in a fiery way. If you want more love, romance, and more beautiful relationships in your life, decide it, choose it. In the same way. Blatantly, consciously, completely, truly, intensely, and in a fiery way. Everything else will be something usual, tepid, and not so direct, fast, useful, or effective. So, choose and decide, decide and choose, and you will move there in every possible way.

> *Fine, I understood that, I will think it over and I will do it! Consciously and 100%, I will decide and choose what I want to experience! Is there any other advice or technique you can suggest in relation to abundance, or romance, love, and personal relationships?*

Yes, many! Stay tuned here and we will be back several times.

FOCUS!

———————— ✳ ————————

Have you noticed how a flashlight focuses its light on a single point in the darkness? This is exactly how our consciousness, our mind, and energy work inside the matter, the possibilities, and potential of life. Or so it can be done.

The "issue" of people is often their focus – or more correctly, the lack of it.

Do you focus? Where do you focus, what do you focus on? How much do you focus on everything, how often, and for how long? Do you focus on what you desire or on the opposite? On what you want or on what you are afraid of?

If you want to experience something, focus exclusively on what you want. Absolutely. Focus your mind, intent, intelligence, perception, creative power, and energy, focus your emotions, choices, decisions, actions. Focus your inner self, your outer self, everything, and anything on the desired experience. Focus now, more and more, focus constantly, more and more. Focus truly, focus completely. Be focused and keep focusing.

Do you want good relationships, friendships, communication, romance, companionship, love? Focus. Focus on love. Focus on love and only on love, focus on love now, focus on love constantly, focus on love absolutely, totally, completely.

Anything else… out! Anything opposite… invalid! Anything smaller or lower… past!

Do you want prosperity, comfort, convenience, free time, quality work, independence, material flow, abundance? Focus. Focus on abundance. Focus on abundance and only on abundance, focus on abundance now, focus on abundance constantly, focus on abundance absolutely, totally, completely.

Anything else… out! Anything opposite… invalid! Anything smaller or lower… past!

Do you desire healing, wellness, strength, vitality, health? Focus. Focus on health. Focus on health and only on health, focus on health now, focus on health constantly, focus on health absolutely, totally, completely.

Anything else… out! Anything opposite… invalid! Anything smaller or lower… past!

Do you desire joy, fulfillment, freedom, peace? Focus. Focus on peace. Focus on peace and only on peace, focus on peace now, focus on peace constantly, focus on peace absolutely, totally, completely.

Anything else... out! Anything opposite... invalid! Anything smaller or lower... past!

Do it for anything you desire to bring, manifest, or experience in your life. Focus all your being, yourself, focus there, right there and only there. Everything else, everything opposite, everything smaller or inferior is past, out, and invalid!

EXERCISE

Declare the following, slowly and calmly, three or more times:

"I focus all of myself, all of my being, my body, and soul, on what I want to experience and only on this! I focus absolutely and supremely on it. I focus my consciousness, intention, mind, emotion, energy, and action on it. I am focusing on it now, right now. I am focusing on it, more and more, constantly and always.

I focus all of myself, all of my being, my body, and soul on .... *(choose and declare what you want: health, love, abundance, peace, joy, positivity, strength, creativity,*

Georgios Mylonas (Geom!*)

completeness, true good relationships, quality work, self-knowledge, self-improvement, happiness, enlightenment). I focus my consciousness, intention, mind, emotion, energy, and action on .... I focus absolutely and supremely on .... I am focusing on .... now, right now. I am focusing on .... more and more, constantly and always."

ASSUMPTIONS, ASSUMPTIONS, REALITY!

EXERCISE FOR HEALTH, PROSPERITY AND GOOD RELATIONS

Assumptions, assumptions, reality...

What would your life be like, if you had and enjoyed health – absolute and perfect health? True health, on all levels, harmony, balance, energy, vitality, and strength. What would your life be like and how would you be? You, your body, your mind, your emotional world? How would you be externally and how internally? How would you feel and what would you experience? What would you choose and what would you do every day? What would you leave, what would you avoid? What would you like and how would you think?

Do this intellectual, mental exercise, and reflect on what your life would be like and how you would be, if you could have and enjoy perfect and absolute health on all levels. Just imagine, just feel, just observe.

And now that you have an idea or, at least, a general sense of how you will be and what your life will be like, think more about this: what do you have to do to get there? What do you need to change or improve, what do you need to leave behind and what new to adopt? Which skills, talents, and characteristics "should" you develop, or express? Which ways of thinking, which habits, which behaviors? Which choices, what daily routine should you have?

Think about it, consider it for a while, in a state of calmness, as much as possible. Without any rush. Just imagine, just feel, just observe.

Apart from health, you can do the same for two other great and vital issues that concern all people. These issues are:

- Abundance, prosperity
- Interpersonal relationships: family, friendship, romance, love

Just consider, think about it:

What would your life be like and how would you be, if you experienced abundance and prosperity?

What would your life be like and how would you be, if you experienced good, true, and beautiful relationships, love, friendship, and romance to a perfect and ideal degree?

What do you need to do to get there? What to leave? How "should" you think? What new habits and attitudes do you need to incorporate into your life, what new gifts and talents do you need to develop and express?

Again, preferably in a state of peace and relaxation, without any rush, choose one of the three areas: health, abundance, and interpersonal relationships.

Bring these questions into your mind and calmly consider them. Dream, imagine. Leave your imagination completely free and fully experience them. As if you are in an alternative state, a very receptive, open, insightful, and intuitive state. In a higher state, a more expanded and intelligent state. Just let yourself go, let yourself go completely.

It is as if you are conversing with a wise part of yourself, with your wise self, the one who —at some point in time and space— lives and experiences what you imagine, envision, and desire.

Feel that such an ideal reality is possible, absolutely possible and close, absolutely close. Feel that you are activated on all levels toward it. That you are inspired, directed, moved toward it. Feel exalted, empowered, grateful, and blissful.

In the following days, do this exercise again. Repetition strengthens it and brings something new, something you may need.

At the same time, during the next days, follow your inner guidance: the one you have received and which you will continue to receive, more and more. Make all the moves and improvements that are necessary and possible, so that the ideal situation that you dream of and envision becomes – as soon and truly as possible – part of your reality.

HEALING A SITUATION

❋

How can I improve certain things in my life? How can I heal a relationship? How can I change or improve my work? How can I improve certain situations, and make them more positive?

Apart from the thought you have to dedicate and the action you have to take, there is an energy method that has the power to bring positivity to every issue and situation in our lives. In family, in relationships, at work, in our emotional state, in our general course. In all and in everything. It is a very simple method and all the great teachers, seekers, and healers have described it, one way or another.

This method is about giving positive energy to the issue that concerns you, instilling positivity in the condition. Bringing light, enlightening. Adding vitality, vital energy, universal or spiritual energy. This raises, uplifts the frequency, the vibration of the situation, but also the experience of it. It changes and transforms. It is a perfect, complete, and whole energy healing technique.

There are many ways to do this technique, many variations, and you can find your own, the one that suits you. Here, I suggest two ways for you.

HEALING A SITUATION: WHITE LIGHT

Bring light to the condition. Light symbolizes positive energy, vital, universal, or spiritual energy, everything good.

First, sit comfortably with your back straight, take a few deep breaths, slowly, deeply, and calmly, and relax, without rushing.

Think about your issue – relationship, work, situation, difficulty, or other issue.

Set the intention in your mind: "Healing of… " (mention the issue).

Imagine that light comes and illuminates your issue.

Bright, clean, white light, healing, light of life, full of love, wisdom, and power.

You can imagine a waterfall of light or a bright floodlight, coming from very high above.

If you cannot imagine it, that is, if you cannot see it as an image in your mind, just assume that it happens. What would it be like if that happened? What would it be like if light illuminated your situation?

Stay for a while with this thought, this intention, this image. Do you feel the heat, the brightness, the energy? Observe!

Then, imagine the situation being healed, improved, or bettered. What would that be like? See it, feel it. Feel the joy, the peace, the relief, the euphoria, the exaltation!

Thank the universe (or the higher power) and open your eyes.

HEALING A SITUATION: GOLDEN SUN

It is a similar method, in which, instead of bringing light/energy into the situation, you place the situation inside the light/energy.

You can do this by mentally placing the situation inside a sun.

Again, first sit comfortably with your back straight, take a few deep breaths, slowly, deeply, and calmly, and relax, without rushing.

Think about your issue – relationship, work, situation, difficulty, or other issue.

Place the intention in your mind: "Healing of... " (mention the issue).

Imagine the situation inside a golden, bright sun. Imagine that it is in its center, in the center of the bright, golden light.

If you cannot imagine it – that is, see it as an image in your mind – just assume that it happens. What would it be like if that happened? That is, if the situation was in a golden, bright sun?

Stay for a while with this thought, this intention, this image. Do you feel the warmth, the brightness, the energy? Observe!

Then, imagine the situation being healed, improved, or bettered. What would that be like? See it, feel it. Feel the joy, the peace, the relief, the euphoria, the exaltation!

Thank the universe (or the higher power) and open your eyes.

Repeat the first or second technique or a combination of both daily, until there is a change.

NEGATIVE
ENERGY – INFLUENCE

———————— ✳ ————————

Someone in my environment is jealous of me. I believe that many of the misfortunes that have happened to me are due to his negative energy. He speaks badly about me and "hoodoos" me! How will I be protected?

Someone envies me and sends me negative energy. What can I do?

From a spiritual point of view, it is not good to give so much power and authority to others over you. It is not beneficial or evolutionary for you. Even if something like this really happens, if someone envies you, thinks or speaks negatively about you, "hoodoos" you or sends you "negative energy," you are allowing it. You are open, vulnerable, and weak in this. Strengthen your energy and place a protective shield around you.

First and foremost, decide and realize that no one and nothing has more power and influence over you than you do. Than yourself. Than you or, if you believe in a higher spiritual power, from this higher element. Only you have the power over you – you control, direct, and dominate your life. Alternatively and additionally, the higher power, whatever name you give it (God, the Divine, Universe, Life, Source of All, etc.), in whatever way you perceive it, understand it or not, has the power over you, it has authority over you. You are its child, its creation. Beloved child and wonderful creation of the supreme and highest universal intelligence of life. You belong to it, you and your life, and that is really ideal and perfect.

You can think and declare something like this:

"Only I have power and authority over me. Over my body, my spirit, my mind, and my soul, over my life. Only myself has power and influence over me. Nothing else can affect me, nothing and no one, it is just impossible!"

Alternatively and additionally, in case you believe that there is a higher power or intelligence (even if it is completely unknown), or if you are just open to this possibility, you can think and say something like this:

"Only the Divine, the Supreme Source, Principle and Power, has power over me. I belong to it completely, we are one. Nothing lower has power over me and can affect me. I have perfect protection, protection on all levels. Absolute protection, Divine protection, everywhere, constantly and always!"

You can do both or just one. But it is not enough to say them mechanically. You need to stop and think about them seriously, reflect on them, process them, and feel them. To believe and internalize them, to make them your own and radiate them. In this way, you give the power, the control, and the ownership of yourself and your life to yourself and to the creative intelligence and power, the source of life that exists within you and everywhere.

Second: Apply some energy and spiritual empowerment techniques.

Visualize a golden sphere surrounding you. A golden sphere of fiery golden light. Powerful, luminous, compact. Like the sun. You are inside it, in its center, and it surrounds you. Imagine it as best as you can, see it mentally and feel it or just assume it happens, that it is reality. As you are in this fiery golden sphere of the bright golden light, affirm that you have perfect protection and that nothing negative can come to you or affect you. "I have perfect protection, perfect protection on all levels. Nothing negative can come to me or affect me! I know it and it is true!"

Do this exercise slowly and calmly, sitting comfortably, with your eyes closed, without rushing. Take a few deep breaths at the beginning and at the end. Do this simple – yet very important – energy technique twice a day, for seven days in a row, in order to see some positive effect and feel the difference. The secret is in repetition.

Negative energy is always around us, as well as confused people with selfish motives. It also exists within us: we are imperfect in our perfection! It is a fact, however, that by increasing our light and power, we can heal both ourselves and our lives, as well as help others to do the same.

MEDITATION RESULTS

I have been doing meditation for a while and, although it relaxes me a lot, I have not seen any specific results. Why?

What results exactly do you expect to see? We do not meditate in order to see a result, but because it is something that is essential, beautiful, and pleasant. For example, when you drink water, do you see any effect? You just need it, your body leads you there and you quench your thirst – it satisfies you. The result of drinking water, the fact that it keeps you alive, is something imperceptible, which happens internally and constantly. Similarly, meditation is the water of the soul. It is daily food for the spirit.

How many wonderful forms and how many elements does meditation have, that make us enjoy it?

Georgios Mylonas (Geom!*)

Being alone, relaxing, becoming calm and tranquil.

Staying still and silent.

Turning inward and upward.

Opening yourself, accepting, letting yourself go.

Breathing deeply, consciously, completely, truly.

Being aware and observing.

Getting in touch with yourself, with your body and mind, with your soul and spirit.

Getting in touch with the source of all, the higher element, whatever name you give it, no matter how you perceive it.

Recognizing and activating the great, hidden power and wisdom that exist within you.

Coming to your center.

Trusting, allowing, flowing.

Praying.

Visualizing.

Illuminating your aura and energy centers.

Opening your heart to love.

Speaking inwardly, positively to yourself, with respect and kindness.

Expressing appreciation and gratitude to All That Is, for the miracle of life and for everything.

Being in tune with the inner aspect of yourself and of the whole existence, your spiritual essence, a dimension of pure light, a field of infinite love, wisdom, and power.

Receiving abundant and pure energy of life, vital energy, this sacred essence, an energy that you feel as a wonderful warmth, you see as an inner light and experience as a peaceful flow, euphoria, and deep nurture.

Strengthening the body internally, supporting, and encouraging its health, renewal, rebirth, and re-creation.

Forgiving.

Releasing.

Emptying your mind and emotions, your psyche from everything negative, inferior, and unnecessary, and being charged again with the superior, beautiful, and positive.

Becoming conscious, becoming aware.

Georgios Mylonas (Geom!*)

Entering alternative, expanded states of consciousness.

Experiencing freedom, wholeness, bliss.

Discovering meaning and purpose in your life, getting direction, knowing who you are - a window to infinity, to the absolute, to the supreme, to the Divine.

Just being yourself, in utter acceptance, fully in the "here and now."

All of these are meditation.

If you read the above slowly and calmly, and made a few pauses in order to reflect or feel them, then you have meditated (if not, you can read them again, slowly and calmly, with this intention)! All these are the infinite results of meditation. They will come and they come more and more with practice. They are probably imperceptible, happening all the time. The direct result is the pleasure you derive, the satisfaction – just like when you drink a glass of water!

VITAL ENERGY
AND HEALTH

---------------------- ✻ ----------------------

What is vital energy? Does it really exist? When does it increase and when does it decrease? How does it help us and how can we have more?

Imagine what it would be like if there was a "magic ingredient" and if your body was filled with it. Filled like an empty vessel with crystal clear water. A hidden element of curing and healing. A secret substance of curing and healing, absolute and perfect. This ingredient does exist and it is life. Life itself. The element of life, the essence of life, the energy of life. It is the pure energy of life, the vital energy.

Vital energy has not been proven and is not yet accepted by science, although no one knows – maybe in the future this may happen, too. It is a theory of the energy arts – "sciences" of the alternative and holistic methods of healing and the inner and spiritual philosophies of self-knowledge, self-improvement, and personal development. A theory supported by great spiritual researchers, exceptional people, and mystics, an esoteric teaching that has a variety of external, practical applications, with many benefits for humans.

The practical applications of the theory of vital energy, very often, bring many good and positive results. Among them, deep relaxation and peace, mental and emotional release, mental clarity and spiritual uplift, empowerment and balance, pain relief and lessening of negative side effects from traditional medical methods and acceleration of healing, in many cases.

Yes, vital energy does exist, although it is invisible to the naked eye, as it happens with thoughts and feelings, which are not visible but are real and true. In the same way, we can experience the vital energy, feel it empirically. We feel it mainly as increased warmth but there are also other sensations related to it, such as flow, cold, a wave, tingling, electricity, vibration, a pulse.

Vital energy is also called life-force energy, bioenergy, etheric energy, or ether. It is the Japanese "ki," as in reiki (rei-ki), which is usually translated as "universal life-force energy." The Chinese "chi," as in the art of tai chi, and the Hindu term "prana," as in pranic healing, also refer to the energy of life. Many associate or equate vital energy with the spiritual light, the spirit, or Holy Spirit of the Christian religion. It is the breath that gives life to all creatures, the power of life.

Vital energy is the "fifth" element of nature, hidden and covered, secret and sacred, invisible and imperceptible, behind and beyond all. You can say that it is a spiritual element or "the" spiritual element. Like all creatures, so we humans receive vital energy indirectly, assimilating it from the other four elements. From the material elements, the elements of nature: earth, water, air, fire. Earth, food, fruits, and vegetables give us this fifth element, the vital energy, in abundance. The water we drink and the air we breathe do exactly the same thing. Sunlight and heat offer us this precious vital energy, too. So we receive our vital energy, the fifth, inner element, from all four, external elements – that is, from the whole of Mother Nature.

Vital energy moves and flows in the energy body of human beings, which is an energy copy of the material, physical, biological body that penetrates and surrounds it. The outer shell of the energy or etheric body is called the "aura," while the basic organs of the energy body are the energy centers – the "chakras." "Chakra" means "wheel" in Sanskrit (the ancient sacred language of Hinduism), as energy centers look like energy vortexes that metabolize energy and channel it to the organs.

There are seven basic and major chakras that connect and affect the body's glands and systems, as well as many secondary centers, throughout the body. At the point where we sit is the first chakra, while at the top of the head is the seventh, with intermediate stations at the second (in front of the pelvis), the third (solar plexus, stomach), the fourth (middle of the chest), the fifth (base of the throat) and the sixth (forehead).

The vital energy, the energy body, and the chakras connect and coordinate the biological body with the other, non-visible but existing fields or levels of the self, its psyche and mind, emotions and thoughts. Thus, vital energy affects – but also is affected – by the body, as well as emotions and thoughts. We can say that the energy body is the link, the bridge between the physical body, the psyche, and the mind, while the chakras are the gates.

Lack of vital energy or blocking its flow at certain points of the body creates imbalance, weakness, negativity and, consequently, disease. Its increase and normal flow provide strength, harmony, vitality, and well-being. There are many ways to increase our vital energy.

First, let's see what reduces or blocks our vital energy:

An unnatural way of life, an inhospitable artificial environment, pollution, conflicts, aggression. Stress, anxiety, negative behaviors, negative thoughts, and negative emotions. Poor diet, heavy or processed foods. Chemicals, alcohol, smoking. The shutdown from what is inside and around us: alienation from the self and alienation from the whole, from existence. The non-expression, the non-acceptance, the non-processing of emotions, thoughts, and traumatic experiences that are hidden, buried, and stored within us. Bad habits and subconscious patterns of negative thoughts, feelings, and choices. A lack of awareness and consciousness.

Now let's see what increases our vital energy:

1. Natural, balanced diet. Rich in vital energy are all fruits, nuts, and vegetables, everything that grows and is offered abundantly by Mother Nature. And, of course, clean water.

2. Contact with nature. Walks and hiking in nature, forests, mountains, by the sea. Swimming. Sun exposure (always in moderation) and fresh air. Caring for animals and plants. It is necessary to be in nature as often as we can and to be in substantial, conscious contact with it.

3. Breath. Not automatic, shallow but conscious, deep breathing. Take ten slow, deep breaths, inhale through the nose, slowly, down to the abdomen and exhale, blowing slowly through the mouth. This breathing instantly and perfectly renews the body, the psyche and the mind, offering abundant, pure,

vital energy. Do it whenever you need it – it is so simple and easy and at the same time the most empowering and invigorating!

4. Sleep: Sleep repairs and rebuilds human beings, in body, mind, and psyche. It is important to enjoy sleep deeply and let ourselves go completely during sleep. A simple relaxation or a short meditation before bed is the best for this purpose. Also, expressing gratitude or focusing on superior, beautiful, positive images, thoughts and feelings.

5. Exercise. Every form of exercise and training stimulates the body but also the mind and psyche. Move your body, so that the vital energy moves but also your life itself!

6. All the inner energy practices and methods, such as reiki, pranic healing, meditation, yoga, tai chi, but also the martial arts increase, unblock, and manage vital energy. Holistic methods such as therapeutic massage, acupuncture, Ayurveda, Chinese medicine, homeopathy, herbal medicine, flower remedies, aromatherapy, and many more do the same.

7. Focusing on higher, good, positive emotions and thoughts provides vital energy and stimulates the energy system. In creative visualization, we imagine ideal images of health (for example) and feel or experience them as much as possible, as if they were reality. This has a positive or even healing effect

on the whole spectrum of our being. Affirmations work similarly and are used by many people to train themselves to turn and focus on the good, the positive, and the useful, and to move more toward it.

8. Laughter and joy. Laughter is highly therapeutic – mentally and physically therapeutic – and is not something we should skip, ignore, or take superficially!

VITAL ENERGY MEDITATION

> *Is there any exercise I can do to increase my vital energy?*

Yes, but first read the previous answer carefully and try to include as many elements from it as you can in your life. Everything is simple, easy, and – mostly – absolutely enjoyable! Remove or reduce what takes away your vital energy and add or increase what gives it to you. At the same time, do the next meditation. To "see some effect," do it twice a day for a few days in a row: for example, morning and evening for seven days in a row. It takes a little practice and – like most things – works best repetitively and cumulatively. Also, whenever you need it, practice this meditation two or three times a day.

How to do the meditation: read it slowly and calmly two or three times and then close your eyes and practice it, as best you can, in your own way, intuitively and freely. But even reading, when it is slow, calm, essential, and you feel it, you feel it deeper, then it is meditation, therefore, as you read the meditation, you can close your eyes every now and then and then apply some of its points.

Energy Exercise for Health: Vital Energy Meditation

Sit comfortably, with your back straight. Gently, close your eyes.

Take ten, slow, conscious, deep breaths. Inhale, slowly and steadily through the nose, down to the abdomen, exhale, blowing slowly and steadily through the mouth. In each inhalation, inhale and fill with positivity and power, everything good. With each exhale, release what you do not need, every tension. Just with your intention. With each breath you feel lighter, more free; with each breath you feel greater calm and serenity. Ten wonderful, full, energetic breaths.

Then, just relax; let yourself go. Mentally, with your intention, enter, in a more receptive, open state, as if you open yourself mentally and energetically, in order to accept everything good, positive, superior.

Imagine that only harmony and peace surround you. Just think of the words: peace, harmony. Peace, harmony, all around, in all directions... Peace, harmony, on all levels. Inside you and around you. Peace and harmony. Absolute, infinite peace. Absolute, infinite harmony. Just imagine what it would be like; just assume it is like that.

Let yourself go even more, relax more, body and mind, mind and body. Relax deeply, relax completely... Let yourself go... Beautiful...

And now imagine what it would be like if there was a sun above your head. A bright sun. Imagine what it would be like if it shed its warm, bright light on you. How wonderful would it be, how perfect. Vital light, vital energy. Feel this energy, this light coming down and entering your body, entering from the top of your head. The vital energy, the vital light slowly and gradually fills the whole body.

Your whole body is filled internally with vital light, pure white light, warm and bright, and you feel more and more weightless and wonderful. Imagine again your whole body full of clean, bright, warm light, full of life and power. See it with your mind. Feel it. Or just suppose that it is happening, that this is the case...

Take a few deep breaths and empower the visualization, make the light even brighter, even whiter, even warmer, more luminous, and more radiant. With each breath, life grows stronger within you, the energy of life increases within you. It is exquisite and amazing, and indeed, it happens.

In order to help and enhance this creative visualization, you can also use the power of speech. That is, in words, express, declare, confirm, either mentally or out loud, what you want and what is happening:

"Light of life! Abundant, pure, vital light all over my body...

Energy of life! Abundant, pure, vital energy, all over my body...

Light of life! Abundant, pure, vital light in every part of my body...

Energy of life! Abundant, pure, vital energy, in every part of my body...

My whole body is alive, clean, bright. Full of vitality, health, and power.

Every part of my body is alive, clean, bright. Full of vitality, health, and power.

My whole body: I recognize it, I appreciate it, I accept it, I love it, and I am grateful for it.

Every part of my body: I recognize it, I appreciate it, I accept it, I love it, and I am grateful for it."

Repeat it three times, mentally or out loud, calmly, slowly and steadily, three times, feeling what you say, meaning it.

Then mentally place, with your thought, a smile on your body. An inner smile. It symbolizes joy, bliss, fullness, strength, awareness, balance, harmony. A big inner smile, then, inside your body. You feel wonderful and exquisite.

Stay silent and peaceful for a while in this expanded, elevated state.

Then, do the same for areas in the body that may be blocked. For any organ or system or part of the body.

Imagine, assume that vital energy, vital light flows toward there. Mentally see or feel (or just keep this thought/intention in mind) the point being filled by this warm, clear, bright light, see and feel the point being illuminated. Being really and fully illuminated. See and feel it clean, bright, and shiny. Clean, bright, and shiny, truly and absolutely.

Help and enhance this creative visualization with an affirmation that confirms what you are doing:

"Light of life! Abundant, pure, vital light in this organ/system/part of my body (you can mention it specifically)…

Energy of life! Abundant, clean, vital energy, in this organ/system/part of my body…

This organ/system/part of my body is alive, clean, bright. Full of vitality, health, and power.

I recognize, appreciate, accept, love, and thank this organ/system/part of my body."

Repeat this three times, mentally or out loud, slowly and steadily, three times, feeling what you say, meaning it. Place mentally an inner smile there as well.

Again, remain silent for a while in this elevated, expanded state.

At the end, see and feel yourself as clean and bright as the sun. You are warm and glowing, radiating power and life. See it and feel it as best you can, as much as you can, and confirm, three times:

"I am absolutely and perfectly healthy. Health throughout the body, health on all levels. Thank you!"

HEALTH ACTIVATION

---- ✳ ----

If you have a health problem, you should always consult a medical professional. Energy techniques work preventively and complementarily. However, they can enhance any healing process internally, in the energy field.

Read the following thought and study it, reflect on it, and feel it. Repeat it three times, out loud, slowly, and calmly, three times. Focus on understanding and feeling what it is saying. Then close your eyes, take ten deep breaths, inhale through your nose, slowly and deeply, exhale, blowing slowly through your mouth. Slowly, deeply, and steadily. With each inhalation, you fill your body with life and positivity. Keep this thought, the intention in your mind, as you inhale. "I breathe life, positivity," or "My body fills with life, positivity."

With your eyes closed, sitting comfortably or lying down, stay calm for a few minutes and observe serenely and silently what is happening, your energy, your body, your thoughts, and feelings. A few minutes are enough. Do this exercise, morning and night, for seven days or more in a row. Preferably, as soon as you wake up and before you go to sleep, when, energetically, you are more open and receptive.

It takes some time to act, like all things in life. If you notice that it helps you, that it actually empowers you toward the health you desire, make it part of your daily routine. You can use it whenever you need extra energy support for health and healing issues.

Energy thought for the activation of our health:

"I activate all the mechanisms that create perfect health, balance, and harmony in my body and make it work properly, ideally, and perfectly.

All the biological, as well as the internal, energy, mental, and psychic mechanisms.

All the material and non-material.

All the known and unknown mechanisms.

I activate all the health mechanisms in my body, now!

I activate all the health mechanisms in my emotion and thought, now!

I activate all the health mechanisms on all levels and aspects of myself, now!

All the mechanisms of perfect self-healing and absolute health are now 'ON' (open, in operation).

The health of my body and spirit, my mind, and my psyche are now 'ON' (open, in operation).

More and more, true health, balance, harmony, wellness, and strength, physically, biologically, and on all levels!

I decide, I choose, I create, I think, I feel, I recognize, I accept, I embrace, I activate and I experience Instant-Perfect Self-healing and Complete-True Health!

Fully aware and with great gratitude, thank you!"

EXERCISE OF ABUNDANCE

———————————— ✺ ————————————

Go to the sea or the ocean. Sit or stand upright. Look at the water. Look at the horizon. And, again, at the water. Take a few deep breaths and relax, calm your inner self, your mind, and emotions. Relax, calm your body. Observe the water. So much quantity, such a perfect essence, so much wisdom and power.

Stay there, looking at the water or the horizon and relax deeply. Relax your body and mind completely, fully, entirely. Peace and harmony, inside and around you, harmony and peace. Open, accept. Look at all this abundance! All this abundance of nature, of life, of the universe, of existence. Truly divine, divine abundance! Contemplate, realize all this abundance, connect, tune into, feel it. Accept more, open more, let go more.

Think and repeat, slowly and calmly, three or more times, mentally – or even better, out loud – meaning and feeling, more and more, what you are saying:

"Abundance, abundance, abundance…

I connect and tune into…

I connect and tune into abundance.

I connect and tune into the abundance of nature, of the universe, of existence, of life.

I connect with the supreme, true, infinite, perfect abundance.

I tune in to the highest, real, unlimited, absolute abundance.

I connect and tune into all this abundance spiritually, mentally, emotionally, energetically, physically.

I tune in and connect with all this abundance from all levels and on all levels.

Abundance, abundance, abundance…

We are one, I am one.

One, now and always, always and now, One."

The beauty, the sweetness of abundance in nature is infinite. The wisdom, the power of abundance in life is perfect. The energy, the joy of abundance in the universe is supreme. The serenity, the fullness of abundance in existence is absolute.

Feel the exaltation, the uplift, and stay in it... without haste, calmly, openly, receptively, peacefully. Enjoy it, assimilate it.

Take it with you, this uplift of true abundance, this abundance of true uplift, take it with you in your daily life. Turn and return to it often!

ABUNDANCE ACTIVATION

———————— ❊ ————————

To activate a greater flow of abundance in your life, abundance of all forms and all kinds, abundance in all areas as well as financial comfort, independence, and prosperity, use the following thought.

Say it, repeat it out loud three times, morning and night, daily for a few days in a row (at least seven). Preferably, as soon as you wake up and before you go to sleep, when, energetically, you are more open and receptive. Slowly, calmly and steadily, meaning and feeling what you say. Then, close your eyes for a while and take three deep breaths, inhaling through your nose, exhaling through your mouth, blowing slowly. Relax and stay in silence for a while, in inner calm, serenity, and self-observation.

In the coming days, become more observant and conscious, observing everything that happens in your life. Do this exercise for at least a week for it to work. If you feel that it helps you, that it unblocks you and mobilizes you internally and externally, then continue it and enjoy the greatest abundance that you create!

"I connect with the Great Abundance!

The Great Abundance that I Am in Reality, the Great Abundance that Life and the whole of Existence Are!

I realize it and I recognize it and I tune more and more into it!

I activate all its forces and gifts, inside me and around me, and I experience it in my daily life and in the here and now, constantly and always!

More and more, true abundance of all kinds and all forms, more and more, true abundance in all areas and on all levels!

I create, I think, I feel, I choose, I decide, I recognize, I transmit, I attract, I receive, I accept and I experience the Great Abundance!

With full awareness and great gratitude, thank you!"

SELF-WORTH

———————— ✳ ————————

What are you worth, how much, and why?

According to the external, social systems in which we live, our value must be acquired. It must be created. It is an external, acquired value: we are worth as much as we do, we are worth as much as we achieve, depending on our work, our achievements. This is what almost everyone, society, the environment, the system, teaches us.

Are you rich, successful? You have worth! Are you hardworking, functional, efficient? You have worth! Are you educated? You have worth! Are you beautiful, strong, healthy? You have worth! Are you likeable, are you good? You have worth! And you can always be more, higher, in all these and worth even more. Yes, all of these are important and can contribute to development and happiness, ours and everyone else's. But they are a level of value, superficial, one side of it, external.

There is another value. Inner, original, authentic, deep. From the core. It is taught without exception by all the great spiritual teachers, all the great inner teachings. According to them, the human being has worth, the human being has worth by itself, the human being has worth himself/herself. You have worth yourself, you have worth as self, as existence. And you not only have worth, you are a value itself. You have worth absolutely, supremely, and perfectly as a value in itself.

You have worth in three ways. First: you have worth just because you are a human being or consciousness, a conscious (or spiritual, if you will) being. Second: you have worth just because you exist or live, you are a "cell" that lives and breathes, a ray of existence that perceives, records, and processes the universe. Third: you have worth just because you are yourself, a separate, special, different, and unique self. No one else is in your place and if you did not exist, right there, there would be a void – whereas now it is something, now it is full, now it is present! Isn't it inconceivably amazing?

So according to the spiritual teachings, a human being has worth truly, completely, absolutely, and perfectly on its own, first of all, "a priori." No matter what it does in the course of its life. It has worth limitlessly and infinitely. Regardless of the course of his/her life, of his/her action, of his/her work, behind it, under it, he/she always has worth.

Nevertheless, one may not know what he/she is worth and how much. One may not know that one is worth it and most likely one actually doesn't know. All evil things derive from this.

Think about it, all the "evil" comes from the often desperate attempts of humans to "have worth": to have worth in their own eyes and others'. To receive recognition, appreciation, acceptance, and even love. To gain prestige, wealth, and goods, to become "better" and "superior." In this effort, they will put on masks and play roles, dress in everything to use it to their own advantage and often against others, as the system is mainly competitive. They will adopt and will be adopted by groups, categories and will try to "belong." I have worth because I belong there – race, nationality, language, religion, social class, origin, area of residence, work, material goods, titles, political party, sports team, appearance – and mine are the best, they are superior, they have worth. These will give them value, borrowed value, external, superficial, temporary.

"We" being against "others" always starts with "I" being against "others." And that is the root of all evil. And it is based on a struggle for the acquisition of appreciation, recognition, acceptance, distinction, prestige, titles, assets, achievements, wealth, a struggle for self-worth.

How different would the world be if every human being consciously knew that one has worth, that one has worth supremely, infinitely, and absolutely? Simply because one lives, simply because one is himself/herself. Simply because life has worth, consciousness has worth. How much is life – consciousness – worth? That much the human being is worth!

When you have worth supremely, infinitely, and absolutely and you know it, then you think, feel, and act accordingly. It is impossible to recognize your own true value – as yourself, as existence, as life – and not recognize it in others. In others, in everyone, in anyone. One automatically derives from the other. If you do not recognize it in others, you have not really recognized it in yourself.

When you have worth and you know it, what you do is never against others. You are not trying to gain value, recognition, appreciation, love, acceptance, prestige, titles, assets, and material goods. You are not trying to acquire, to win. Whatever you do, you do it from a different point. Because you love it, from a point of love, completeness, calm. Expressing your value, the value of life, of existence, through you. Everything else comes naturally and easily, in abundance and so simply. It is a different existential point, where you feel good. If you have self-knowledge, you have self-value. If you have self-value, you have self-knowledge.

This does not mean that you do not move, do not act, do not create, or that you do not "belong" to groups or categories. But you do not identify, you do not use them against others, and you do not draw self-worth, as if you do not have one. You do not hook, you do not depend, you do not cling onto anything. Like everyone else, you face a variety of "issues" and a variety of "challenges." But you face them from another – freer, more conscious, more serene, more complete – point.

If we all lived that way, as values in themselves, that deserve absolutely, supremely, and perfectly, how different would the world be? How much would it change?

EXERCISE: I HAVE WORTH

This exercise, in one way or another and in various variations, is often done in workshops and groups of personal development. It focuses on recognizing our inner, deeper self-worth, the fact that we have worth. When we realize and understand this in all its range and truth, we gain great peace and tranquility and we can choose direction, action, and work in our lives more fully and more freely. We are not interested in "proving" our self-worth. We just have it, we transmit it, we share it.

Say "I have worth!" Say it mentally and, if you dare, say it out loud… "I have worth!" Did you dare? Again. "I have worth!" Do you feel the vibration? The energy of the word? It is strong, it shakes you. Repeat. "I have worth!" If you cannot do it, do it as a game, as a theatrical role. It will make it easier for you and will have a positive effect.

Also, read the following and repeat it a few times. Think about it, reflect on it, meditate on it, and adopt it, assimilate it completely inside you, make it your truth.

"I have total worth. I have supreme worth. I have infinite worth. I am worth having worth. I love my worth, I respect it, I recognize it, I appreciate it. I share and emit it, I express it, and I transmit it. Easily, abundantly, naturally, simply! I recognize the highest and perfect value of all life and existence! Of all human beings and all creatures. Behind the veil, behind the masks, all are values in themselves, all have worth and have worth absolutely, supremely, and infinitely. And simply for that reason, I recognize, appreciate, respect, and love humans and all creatures! They exist, so they have worth. I exist, so I have worth."

You exist, so you have worth.

LOVE AND ACCEPTANCE
OF OURSELVES

"I love and accept myself."

A highly healing exercise. Healing internally, energetically, mentally. An essential exercise, of essence, an exercise of life, vital. Myriad of problematic issues arise from lack of love and acceptance of ourselves by ourselves. And myriad good things, when it is true and real.

Bring the following thought to your mind: "I love and accept myself. I truly love me. I accept myself fully, deeply, completely."

What does that look like? Do you think it is ridiculous? Do you think that it is not true? Do you think it is unnecessary? Do you think it is distant? Do you think it is difficult? Or do you think it is "selfish"? All these indicate that you need to believe it, to experience it, to make it true, your own, your truth, and your reality. The more ridiculous, untrue, unnecessary, distant, difficult, or "selfish" it seems to you, the more necessary it is!

Full and deep acceptance and true and pure love for ourselves is essential, necessary, and vital for a balanced personality, for a balanced psyche. Full and deep acceptance and true and pure love for ourselves is essential, necessary, and vital in order to experience fully, deeply, truly, and clearly other people and life itself.

It is not selfishness, it is rehabilitation, healing. It is not selfishness, it is selflessness, altruism. By healing ourselves, our personality, and our psyche – through love and acceptance, which work only positively and make everything possible – we can help others, from another, better, more balanced point. From the point of love and acceptance.

So it is time to do it seriously. Truly. Focused. Fully.

Sit down and repeat the phrase. "I love and accept myself. I truly love me. I accept me fully, deeply, totally." Slowly and calmly. And wait. Repeat. Wait. Try to understand what you are saying, to feel it, what it would be like if it were completely true. Repeat. Wait and observe.

Repeat mentally, or even better out loud.

Do it until there is some feeling, some effect, some reaction. There may be an emotional reaction or you may have images or thoughts, or even a physical reaction. You may feel some kind of blockage or burden or something else. You may cry or yawn. Do not stop. Take a deep breath – and maybe a few more – and continue. Calmly, focused, with willpower.

You may also enter into another state of consciousness: for example, you may feel great joy or euphoria, exaltation or expansion, deep peace or tranquility. Or release and purification.

Do this exercise for a few minutes, without rushing. The more substantially and truly, the greater the positive effect it will have inside you, energetically and mentally, but also around you, since the "inside" always affects the "outside."

Repeat for a few days, until it becomes a reality, until it "enters" your cells! It is extremely beneficial and transformative.

"I Love and Accept Myself. I Truly Love Me. I Accept Me Fully, Deeply, Totally."

OPENING OF THE HEART: EMOTIONAL HEALING

We all have been hurt or are being hurt. Emotionally and on all levels. From others, from the difficult, unpleasant experiences of life, and from ourselves. We are imperfect, limited beings (or so we believe and feel) that function, most of the time, unconsciously and without awareness. They betray us, they judge us, they belittle us, they deceive us, they attack us, they fight us, they hurt us. And we do the same to others, but also to ourselves. We criticize and judge others and ourselves and are often harshly critical or critically harsh. We think negatively, we feel negatively, and we talk negatively about life, about people and about ourselves. Not always, but often or even sometimes. Not completely consciously but, mainly, subconsciously.

The result is that we get hurt and our hearts close. Our energy heart closes energetically. It shrinks, weighs, thickens, darkens. Imagine, if you can, the energy of a weak, sick, hurt, closed person who does not trust himself/herself, others, and life. And the energy of a strong, healthy, open person, full of life, joy, peace, and love, who trusts, lets himself/herself go, accepts, and flows abundantly, naturally, and freely. Imagine, if you can, their energy difference. How they are, how they look like, what they emit, as quality, as frequency.

When the heart closes, our energy is negatively affected and our health is burdened, on all levels: mentally and emotionally, energetically, and biologically. When it is open, clean, and bright, everything works properly, perfectly, and ideally. There is flow, harmony, and balance.

In some people, their hearts are very closed. They experience life to a small degree, at a low level, very limited, without meaning and joy. They cannot give or receive love, and possibly nothing essential or good. For most people, the heart closes at certain times when something bad happens or when they go through a difficult phase. This is human and natural and simply means that it is time for healing. For a new opening or for more opening of their heart, for its purification, a positive charge, and illumination, for its renewal and rebirth. It is time for change, turn, return, ascension, and exaltation to the best we can be and experience.

Each person can open the heart more. Heal it, strengthen it, elevate it, enlighten it even more. The energetic heart: it is located in the center of the chest and is the one that receives and emits every emotion. Pain and anger, sadness and fear, bitterness and grief, and on the other hand, joy and hope, optimism and tranquility, bliss, and peace.

Many people are afraid of opening their heart, while closing is what they should be "afraid of" – avoiding or correcting it when this happens. Living with a closed heart is living without joy but also without trust, something that is particularly difficult and painful. When you live with an open heart, you have trust and, therefore, joy. It is natural for your trust to diminish or be lost when the others hurt you, when you are hurt, but you are the final responsible for your life, you are the primary being responsible for its reconstruction. Trust is essential – vitally essential for a deep, meaningful, and complete life experience.

Negative emotions and traumatic, unpleasant, painful experiences close the human heart in an effort for self-protection and avoidance of pain. It is a natural instinct, but from there we need to move forward; work and healing need to be done, as this is not the ideal situation for us humans.

An open heart does not mean that you are a vulnerable person. It does not mean that you are more open to pain or negativity, anger, fear, sadness. It means that you are in contact with yourself, in contact with the great wisdom, power, and love that you have within you, that life provides you, abundantly, spontaneously, and naturally. This opening makes you not only full of love, but also a wiser, stronger person. That is, you have the opportunity to experience the possible negativity and difficulties, with more wisdom and more power. To cope more easily, to face, to accept, to understand, to transmute, to heal, to release and to disengage, to overcome and transcend. More easily and faster. This is desirable and important!

You become a more complete and fuller being, you become a wiser and stronger being, when your heart is open. "Your heart is open" means that your core is active, your center is active, yourself, you are active.

- A closed heart:

- Does not accept and cannot give, does not receive and does not transmit. It does not accept and therefore does not offer joy, love, and care.
- Does not allow us to experience what is worthwhile, what we really want: peace, tranquility, freedom, bliss, and fullness.

- An open heart:

- Is in communication with ourselves, the true self. Body, mind, spirit, and soul in coordination, harmony, and unity.
- Communicates with others. Creates authentic relationships, attracts more positive people, and creates better situations.

- Communicates with the higher element, the divine, with existence, and life itself. It discovers and experiences meaning, value, purpose, depth, breadth, and height in everything. It guides us spiritually, it is our inner compass.

- When do you need to "open your heart"?

- When you face a difficult situation.
- When you have gone through or are going through a traumatic experience.
- When you are hurt.
- When you have lost the joy.
- When you need more harmony, calm, and serenity.
- When you feel that you are in negativity, in an empty, blank, closed or heavy state.
- When you are stuck in unpleasant emotions such as fear, frustration, anger, and sadness.
- When you have lost your confidence or your direction.
- When you cannot connect essentially, communicate genuinely with others.
- When you do not know what you really want.

- Why open your heart?

Opening the heart has benefits and only benefits. Open your heart to:

- Discover the power within you, the joy of life
- Awaken your emotional and energy "immune system"
- Enhance your health
- Cope with any difficulty, with more wisdom and awareness
- Empower yourself on all levels: energetically, mentally, emotionally, physically, and spiritually
- Find again the confidence inside and outside yourself, the confidence in yourself and the environment
- Reconnect with yourself, with others, with the whole, existence and life.

- What opens our hearts?

These open and heal the heart:

Love, care, interest.
Friendship, good company, true, meaningful
    communication.
Contact, touch, hug, kisses.
Romance.
Nature, frequent and conscious contact with nature.

Sun, fresh air, greenery, flowers, trees, water, sea.

Breathing, when it is conscious, substantial, slow, full, deep.

Plants, contact with plants and their care.

Animals, contact with animals and their care.

Children, playing with children and their care.

Games, laughter.

Art, beauty, creativity.

Music, singing.

Exercise, body movement.

Massage, in all its therapeutic kinds.

Counseling and psychotherapy work, understanding and regaining self-confidence, inner strength.

Inner, spiritual study and work, understanding of the human nature.

Positive thinking and positive emotions, joy, peace, tranquility.

Prayer, when done from the soul.

Meditation.

Energy therapies such as reiki and energy practices such as yoga.

Holistic healings.

Compassion, selflessness, offering to others.

ENERGY EXERCISES FOR OPENING THE HEART

Adopt and incorporate the above, as much as you can, into your life. Is there anything you would like to do that you have not done yet? Begin now!

At the same time, here are some energy exercises that will immediately help you to open your heart wide again to positivity and all the good things you want to experience and which you really deserve!

Instructions: Do the following exercises several times repeatedly, such as twice a day and for a few days in a row – for example, seven consecutive days – to see and experience some substantial – energy and emotional – difference. You can do any exercise that expresses you or some combination of them, or all four exercises, one after the other. Of course, they can also be combined with the techniques that follow.

* First Exercise: "Open the window!"

Start by taking a deep breath.

Affirm the following, slowly and calmly, three times, mentally or out loud:

"My heart opens, it opens more and more and this is safe and good for me. I activate – here and now – its complete awakening, the perfect cleansing, the complete healing, and its true enlightenment."

Close your eyes and imagine that there is a window in the middle of your chest. Feel the window open wide, as if you were opening its shutters outward, to get plenty of fresh air and plenty of sunlight. Stay this way and observe, with the window in your chest open, completely open. Assume, imagine, feel that fresh air and warm light, pure positivity, and abundant life enter inside you.

Focus on good, superior, positive emotions, such as trust, love, joy, serenity, harmony, peace, freedom, fullness, gratitude. Say these words and enter into their experience. Feel their energy, feel and experience them, as much as you can. Calm, relaxed, without pressure, without haste. Trust, love, joy, peace, harmony, tranquility, freedom, fullness, gratitude...

After a while, take a deep breath and complete, stating three times, slowly, mentally, or out loud:

"My heart is truly open, fully awake and completely pure! Healed, enlightened, bright! I am safe, happy, connected, and trusting myself again, others, existence, and life."

* Second Exercise: "Look how it blooms…"

You can start with a deep breath and a positive statement, using the confirmation of the first exercise.

Imagine that in the middle of the chest there is a beautiful rose or some other beautiful flower. Imagine that it is opening its petals, blooming. One by one its petals open, one by one all the petals open. Then, feel the rose open, blooming, alive. Shiny, sweet, aromatic, colorful, intoxicating. It radiates energy, light, life. Exquisite, divine!

As in the first exercise, think and focus on positive emotions and imagine them, feel them, get into the energy, into their experience, as much as you can, as much as possible, for a few minutes.

Close with a deep breath and a positive statement, like the last confirmation of the first exercise.

* Third Exercise: "The sun inside you!"

Take three slow, full, deep breaths and let go completely, relax your body and mind completely.

Assume that there is a sun in the center of your chest. Imagine it and feel that it is emitting its warm, golden light. Can you imagine it, can you feel it? The sun in the center of your chest spreads its warm, fiery light. It radiates wonderful light of life, exquisite vital light all over the chest. Observe it... The sun radiates this pure positivity throughout your body. It is real and it happens, it happens and you feel it more and more. It is an amazing experience.

The sun symbolizes the spiritual source within us, our spiritual core, the higher, the deepest element, the divine. Connect with it, awaken to it, activate it.

Repeat three times, slowly and calmly, out loud or mentally:

"Love, wisdom, power...

I activate the true love, the true wisdom, and the true power of my true self...

I activate the deepest love, the deepest wisdom, and the deepest power of the deepest source within me...

I connect, I recognize, I experience, I manifest, I express...

Higher, Supreme Love... Higher, Supreme Wisdom... Higher, Supreme Power...

Unlimited, Infinite Love... Unlimited, Infinite Wisdom... Unlimited, Infinite Power...

Absolute, Perfect Love... Absolute, Perfect Wisdom... Absolute, Perfect Power...

Thank you…"

Take three deep breaths, slowly and calmly, and the exercise is complete.

* Fourth Exercise: "With the hand on the heart…"

Put your palm, whichever one you want, on your chest and take a deep breath.

Slowly and calmly, say the following, inside you or even better out loud, three or more times:

"I open my heart to love. I open my heart to trust. I open my heart to joy. I open my heart to myself. I open my heart to others. I open my heart to All That Is. I open my heart to life. It is safe for me. It is good for me. It is wise and powerful. True and essential. I want it, I realize it, I choose it and I do it, now and always. It happens immediately, easily, simply, naturally."

Between repetitions, take a deep breath. At the end, take another deep breath. Stay for a while and observe. How do you feel?

OTHER ENERGY TECHNIQUES

* Taps: "Open Sesame!"

There are three simple movements that open and activate the heart immediately and which are so effective! Try all three. Do them whenever you need empowerment and awakening in the energy center of your heart.

1. Do small taps with your fingers or with your palm closed in the middle of the chest. Not forcefully. At whatever speed you think is right, experiment with it. Do it for about a minute. Stop and observe the point.

2. With both palms, make a movement as if you are opening your chest. Starting from the middle of the chest, pulling with the fingers outward. Repeat a few times. Stop and observe the point.

3. With the whole palm, do a circular rub on the chest, with whichever palm and in the direction that you feel better and prefer. Do it a few times. Stop and observe the point.

Before doing the above movements, place your intention at the beginning: "Awakening of the heart" or "I open my heart." Think about it or say it out loud a few times and make the movements. At the end, mentally or out loud, confirm: "My heart is awake" or "My heart is open."

Georgios Mylonas (Geom!*)

* Positive Affirmations

It is known that thought influences and directs energy and emotion. Speaking, expressing your thought even more so.

Write ten positive affirmations about emotional healing, opening of the heart. Write them in your own words, simply. They have to be absolutely positive and in the present tense, so that you can confirm something good and wonderful in the "now." Although what you write will be ideal, it will be what you want to achieve, what you want to experience. For example:

"I open my heart.
I heal my heart.
I overcome and release the past.
I focus and enjoy the present.
I accept and welcome the future – it is getting better, brighter, and more positive.
I renew myself mentally and emotionally.
I open my heart to joy and trust.
I open my heart, completely and truly.
Peace and joy in my heart, always peace and joy and only peace and joy!
I accept love and offer love, I accept and offer freely, abundantly, spontaneously!
I release whatever I do not need, I move on and now I move to the joy, the flow, and the ease!

I open up, I rejoice, I connect, I trust, again and again,
    more and more!
I am always well and I am always safe.
There is inexhaustible wisdom, love, and power within me.
I deserve only good, I deserve all the good.
I face everything with love, wisdom, and strength."

Write your own positive statements too. You can use the above but it is even better to write some of your own. Write them down and read them over and over again, slowly and calmly. Try to understand what you are saying and feel it. As if it is true, as if it is happening now. Stay for a while in peace and tranquility, in silence, internally, in the energy, and in this state. How is it? Feel opening, expansion, elevation and exaltation, renewal and empowerment, and smile deeply!

* Energy Breaths

Sit comfortably, with your back straight. Take ten deep breaths, ten energy breaths. Inhale through the nose, slowly, steadily, and deeply, down to the abdomen. Exhale through the mouth, blowing slowly and steadily.

Before inhaling, think, say mentally or, even better, out loud: "I open my heart."

Then do the slow and deep inhalation-exhalation. Repeat this thought-intention and do the breath again. Do three such breaths.

Then, think, or say mentally or out loud: "My heart is open!" Again, inhalation and exhalation. Three times, with the same thought at the beginning.

Finally, think and say: "Opening to joy, I am open to joy" or "Opening to trust, I am open to trust" or "Opening to love, I am open to love."

Do four deep breaths with this thought in mind at their beginning.

In total, they are ten slow, full, deep breaths. The exercise is complete. Stay a little in silence and tranquility and observe yourself internally. How do you feel?

OTHER GREAT IDEAS

While the Logos, the thought, the intention, is the main ingredient and the driving force in order to create everything, not only in energy but also in matter (really, what can you create without focus and intention?) and while all the power and wisdom is within us, there are some elements of nature that we can add to our lives to improve it. We can see them as complementary tools, as external aids, as gifts of nature, for the healing of the human being on all levels. The external elements of nature, combined with the inner power of speech and thought, focus and intention, enhance any therapeutic or other work. So, just open up and trust the wonderful power of nature!

* **Aromatherapy**

The essential oil of rose, with its heavenly aroma, is considered ideal for opening the heart. You should always be careful that it is not a synthetic fragrance but a clean, pure, natural essential oil.

As it is super-super-concentrated, particularly rare and expensive, rose essential oil is usually sold dissolved in another oil, in a base oil, such as almond or jojoba oil. There are bottles that have the percentage written on them of how much rose essential oil they contain – it is usually 3% or 5% or 10% rose in almond or jojoba oil or other base oil. Sometimes, instead of base oil, it may also be dissolved in alcohol. In the rare case that you have insoluble, neat, pure, super-concentrated essential oil, add a drop (yes, one drop is enough!) into a base oil, so that you can dilute it and be able to use it.

With this oil, which will contain the rose essential oil, gently massage it on your chest, putting several drops in your palm. Massage for a few minutes and then relax, feeling, experiencing its effect. Alternatively, add a few drops in a tub of warm water, and immerse yourself in it. Relax for 10-20 minutes. Additionally, if you want, add two to three handfuls of coarse sea salt for an extra energy cleansing! Do one of the two practices three days in a row and feel your heart blossom with care, warmth, and love!

You can also combine rose essential oil with lavender, mixing a few drops of each, since lavender is also an excellent oil for healing, bringing increased peace and harmony on all levels.

Caution: Essential oils should not be used during pregnancy and, in case of a health problem, users should first consult their doctor. Keep away from children and pets and always use externally (they are not drinkable). Carefully read the instructions for use on the packaging.

* Crystal Therapy

The crystal of pure love is none other than rose quartz. Place a rose quartz – after you cleanse, charge, and activate it – in the middle of your chest. Hold it gently there and relax for a few minutes. You can also further activate the center of the heart by holding the crystal and doing circles with it in front of your chest. Do it slowly and calmly. Experiment with the direction, counterclockwise or clockwise. Do it in both directions, several times in each direction before you change to the other. If the crystal has a vertex, tip or point (called a "laser" or "wand" crystal), turn and hold the point toward your body to direct and focus the energy there.

As you do the above techniques, keep in mind your intention, knowing "why" you do them. The intention is either: opening of the heart, cleansing, or healing of the heart. Or focus on the word "love," on the meaning, the energy of love.

Bring the intention "opening and healing of the heart" or the word, the meaning and the energy of love in your mind, at the beginning and at the end of the exercise but also during the exercise. Calmly, slowly, internally.

To feel or see substantial results, do this exercise for a few minutes each day, a few days in a row – for example, seven days in a row.

Apart from rose quartz, all pink and green crystals are ideal for treating the heart's energy center. Among them you may use the following: malachite, aventurine, amazonite, cyanite, green tourmaline, pink tourmaline, chrysocolla, rhodochrosite, chrysoprase, kunzite, peridot, emerald. So, open yourself to the love of crystals, the love of the earth, and ground the crystal love that you have inside you!

The methods for opening the heart are completed here. Now it's time to practice them; it's time for action.

Let us wish good, wonderful, and true opening to the pure, bright, and full of love, wisdom, and power, heart of all! And let us wish good, wonderful, and true opening to your pure, bright, and full of love, wisdom, and power, heart!

Remember: human beings deserve to live openly. That is, with joy and trust in themselves, others, and life. They deserve it, they really deserve it, and they absolutely deserve it.

Remember: you deserve to live openly, with joy, with trust in yourself, others, and life. You deserve it, you really deserve it and you absolutely deserve it…

And whenever you forget it, remind yourself again:

"I deserve to live openly. With joy, with trust in myself, in others, and in life. I deserve it, I truly deserve it, and I absolutely deserve it!"

FEAR: UNDERSTANDING
AND RELEASING

———————— ✳ ————————

> *How can I overcome fear? I feel that it immobilizes me and does not help me develop as a person. Sometimes I have a general, vague fear, an anxiety, and other times I have a strong fear of insignificant things.*

I have good and bad news: it depends on how you see it! But I suggest you see it as good, as an opportunity for understanding and awareness, but also for healing and development.

Fear is egoism. Or, to be more precise, fear is often excessive egoism. Unnecessary and meaningless fear, without any immediate and obvious cause of threat, is egoism. Disguised egoism. The more you fear, for no reason, the greater your egoism, and the greater your egoism, the more you fear in vain, in vain and unnecessarily.

Fear is a completely natural and instinctive mechanism that every person has inside. It protects us and makes us feel safe. Fear is an instinct, but, at the same time, it is learned. Your hand is burned and you are afraid of fire. You are afraid of it, you avoid it, you are safe. The environment and family prevent you, stop you, and warn you, and thus you are afraid to do several things to be safe, alive, healthy, and stay that way. But what happens when fear grows extremely and takes control?

I cannot give you psychological advice; you should visit a mental health counselor, psychologist, or psychotherapist for this issue if you do not see improvement. I can only give you spiritual or energy directions.

When we human beings do not develop our talents, wisdom, and power, when we do not develop the "upper," then the "lower" takes control; our lower side, our bad or negative side – as we feel it this way, unpleasant and negative. Fear is the master of this side; it dominates and controls. When we are possessed by fear we are deprived of life. The life we want and which we can live. When we are in fear we do not want and cannot live. Live truly, totally, with breadth and in depth and in height. We reduce ourselves to a minimum, we feel scared, weak.

We, human beings are trapped in something that is not true, because we are not really weak. It is an illusion, a strong mental belief: I am weak. We believe it with all our power, we have recorded it and we experience it as a reality. Our ego, our egoism (the part that says "I want to be well," "I want to feel good," and "I, above all!"), uses fear to achieve what it wants: to feel good, to be well. Protected, safe. Stable, stable in the past, in the known, in the same. Stable and comfortable even in something negative, as long as we know it; this makes us feel secure.

And fear at the same time uses our lower side, the ego, to perpetuate its energy, its beingness, its existence. Fear says to ego: "Yes, you are fine with me here, I keep you safe. Do not do, do not dare, do not speak, do not go… Stay still, speechless, unsmiling, here. It is the best for both!" Thus, fear and ego, fear and lower self, a dark alliance, often command the human psyche, mind, body, life.

Fine, I've now told you the "bad news" about fear and ego. But I also have good, very good, the best possible news. When you realize the "game" that is being played within you, the game that you are playing, as ego and as fear, you can stop it. You can exceed it and overcome it. You can reduce and correct it. You can illuminate and heal it. How can you heal something you do not see it exist? But when you see it, a new possibility opens up.

So, recognize fear as a childish "game" of your ego, so that it feels good, feels safe, without a cause, without a threat (without the danger of fire, that is). Now feel that there is another aspect inside you. It is another aspect, different and independent, to which they give many names. Keep what you like, what suits you. Your other aspect is your "upper," your "upper" side. It is brighter, airier and sunnier, more pleasant. It is called the true self or higher self. It is called spirit or soul. It is called light. Love. Inner power, inner wisdom. In other words, it is your potential, your greatest potential.

It is located above the ego and is a wiser and stronger part of you. And not only that, it is also above the ego in the sense that it is more you. It is more you than the ego is you. And you are more of this than you are the ego. Do you understand? You are more your upper aspect than you are your lower. You are more the deeper, the higher self, the light, the love, the wisdom, the power, the spirit, your soul, than you are your ego. Even if your ego tells you "I am you and you are nothing else!"

To understand it even better, imagine a large circle, bright, full of love, wisdom, and strength. That is you. The big, higher self. The spirit, the soul. Your potential, your greatest potential. Nice. Now, in this big circle, in its center, imagine a smaller circle. The lower self (in relation to the big one). The "ego." Limited, small, insecure, scared. It shouts, "Here

I am! Can't you see me? Me! I want, I need! I am you!"
Without realizing it, although you are the big circle that
includes the small, you have completely identified only with
the small. You have entered a small and somewhat dark
room, full of fear, the room of your ego. And you have
probably closed both the door and the windows. To the
light, love, wisdom, power, to this greater being that you are.

When you think about it and understand it, when you
realize it, the fear automatically decreases, and many times
it evaporates, disappears. When you open the windows, the
light enters abundantly and the darkness disappears; love,
wisdom, and power automatically cancel out the fear.

Again, I am not referring to the natural fear that protects
you from the fire and all the dangers, that keeps you alive,
healthy, and safe. I'm not referring to this fear, but to the
additional, to the unnecessary, the unjustifiable, the useless,
the excessive, the unbalanced. The one that the ego, in its
unknowingness and weakness, uses in order to feel good.

Think about it well and deeply, process it, and meditate on
it. Get out of the small, gloomy, dark room. Believe firmly
and feel in your cells the greatest power and the deepest
wisdom that you really are and decide to live life in its full
form, in its full completeness. To live life with light and love,
with wisdom, and power, with soul and spirit. Higher and
bigger. With perfect confidence and absolute safety. Not
with darkness, not with egoism, not with fear.

Georgios Mylonas (Geom!*)

Think, ponder, meditate and open, recognize, accept. Decide, choose and confirm, affirming with courage, intensity, faith, and passion, as often as you need it:

"I know that unnecessary, useless, unjustifiable, and aimless fear comes from my ego, from the lower, limited part of myself.

I recognize it and I realize it.

It is an effort to feel good and safe.

But in reality, I am completely safe.

I recognize and realize that this fear means that I have stayed, that I have been trapped/shut inside my ego.

I need to open up, be more receptive, and gain perfect trust.

I take a decisive brave step, full of courage and boldness, and I open again to my biggest self, to my biggest beingness, full of wisdom, and power.

I tune in to my bright and beloved center, full of freedom, peace, and fullness.

I open it, recognize it, tune in, and get into it.

More and more, I release everything I do not need, constantly, I release anything unnecessary.

I have the power and wisdom to choose consciously and truly, who I am and what I experience, even more each day.

I decide and choose to go beyond fear and, with complete receptivity and trust, to experience complete security, the deepest power, the source of joy and the undisturbed peace, which I absolutely deserve and in fact I am."

REHAB "CLINICS"

Negativity is a drug. A regular, real drug. An addictive substance. Negativity, whatever meaning one gives it, has all kinds and forms. Human beings depend on it and ask for it in every way, just like the drug addict – after all, are drugs not a form of strong negativity? Drug addicts cannot live without them – at least this is what they believe and feel. They depend on it on all levels, mentally-emotionally but also energetically-physically. Taking drugs makes them feel good, euphorically; it offers them pleasure and tranquility, even for a while, before they fall again into needing and desiring it.

Negativity comes on a spectrum: negative situations and problems, negative actions and negative energies, and even more, negative thoughts and negative emotions. Individual and collective negativity, personal and interpersonal, social and global, conscious and subconscious, obvious and disguised. It works just like a drug. It drugs you, puts you to sleep, numbs you, desensitizes you. It blurs the mind, the judgment, and the psyche. It absorbs your energy and destroys your body. It makes you lose yourself, forget who you are, your power. Negativity offers a superficial sense of self, a borrowed self-worth, false sense of security, and minimal, temporary power.

Have you ever felt intense anger or hatred? Have you ever felt intense fear or sadness? Have you used violence of any kind? Then you know empirically that all these forms of negativity raise the adrenaline and wake up all your systems. They make you feel alive, you decompress, you express yourself. You feel you have reached a higher point than before, important and special. After this intensity, although negative, you experience temporary peace and contentment, even joy or euphoria.

In the future, there will be rehab "clinics" for negativity. It is necessary, they must be created and it will happen. Or do they already exist? Yes, they actually exist already, they have existed for a long time and will always exist in the future. The rehab "clinics" for any kind of negativity are called "spiritual teachings." Spiritual teachings, whatever one may mean, of all kinds and forms. They are the rehab of human beings from negativity, from every kind and from every form of negativity.

All spiritual teachings have a common baseline at their core, a common essence, a common purpose: the rehab and liberation of human beings. Their enlightenment, their happiness. To offer them a better relationship with themselves, with their environment, with Life and with Existence, with the Whole. A more true, deep, meaningful, conscious relationship. They are the tools, the means, the paths to freedom and the fullness that human beings deserve and can experience.

As in all cases of drugs, of addictive substances, it is not something that is simple or easy. It is a constant struggle of life and it is the battle that human beings fight for life itself. It is the only battle that is really worth fighting and which one must fight with all their power.

EXERCISE:

If you see and feel that it expresses you, try saying the following. Make it a part of your daily routine, whenever you need it, to confirm, reinforce and express a new – improved, better, more conscious – option for you.

"I choose rehab from negativity. I detox myself from all forms of negativity. Complete and perfect detoxification from all the inferior, unpleasant, negative emotions, thoughts, and patterns. I disengage myself, I am released, I unhook myself, I unblock, I transcend, I am healed, and I heal. With every breath. Liberation and freedom, now and constantly. Liberation and freedom, everywhere and always.

I recognize and totally rediscover my true self. I choose who I am and what I experience. I am free, I am full, and I experience freedom and fullness, emotionally and mentally, on all levels and in all areas of my life. I have all the power and wisdom to do it and I do it – simply, easily, directly, spontaneously, naturally."

VIOLENCE AND UNPLEASANT SITUATIONS

—————— ✳ ——————

I read in various spiritual books that we must have love, be good, have positivity, faith, persistence and patience, spiritual virtues, in order to progress and develop spiritually and to be well, happy, as much as possible. Should I, out of love, live in a relationship or a situation that is unpleasant? Somewhere where there is a lie, dishonesty, where they do not show me respect and appreciation? In a situation where there is physical, verbal, or psychological oppression, or even violence? Either this violence happens to me, I am the victim, or I witness what happens to someone else or to others. Do I have to accept it, tolerate it, and show patience, tolerance, and love? Should I forgive, forget, and overcome whatever happens, whatever they do to me?

No. This is not love; it is stupidity. It is not patience, persistence, tolerance, spirituality, kindness. It is not forgiveness. It is stupidity, pure stupidity. I know, you do not like the word. But that's it; it is not possible to use another word in its place: stupidity. But it is something really good, if you recognize it, it does not belittle you, nor does it offend you. On the contrary, it increases you and honors you completely.

If you tolerate a negative situation, oppression, and violence, if you are not appreciated and respected, then where is the respect, appreciation, and love for you, for yourself? If you do not appreciate, respect, care for and do not love yourself, then you do not truly love others. You live and function only from the level of a troubled, deficient, unbalanced personality, who fakes love. A love that you don't have, a love that you don't know, a love that you have not experienced, and a love that you are not yourself.

So where is the love for you, for yourself, but also where is the love for the other person? How do you love the other person, when you allow him/her to have and continue to have such a behavior? This is not love; it is stupidity. You do not really respect and appreciate the one you allow and make it easier for him/her to be his/her worst self. You allow, continue, and perpetuate negativity and evil. By making space and giving your presence and energy, you participate.

You just pretend to love him/her. You pretend that you forgive, that you respect and that you appreciate.

It is natural to pretend, since you do not have love. And you have no love for the reason I've mentioned: you are not in love with – in the energy and essence of love, having left your most central and important part outside – yourself. Simply put, you do not have love because you do not love, do not respect, and do not appreciate the closest, most personal and intimate person, the one you were born with, the one you walk with, the one you constantly live and breathe with: yourself, you. When you exclude yourself from your love, there is no one left to love.

It is stupidity. I know you do not like that word. It hits you, it makes you angry, it offends you. But let it just move you, shake you, wake you up, arouse you. Just because a situation or behavior is stupidity, it does not mean that you are stupid. It is not just stupid people who do stupid things. The rest do, too; everyone else does. Both wise people and spiritual people. The wise, spiritual beings. And this is what you really are, in your essence. A wise, spiritual being.

Yes, it may sound strange to you. But you are. "Appearances can be deceptive," don't you know? You may not see it, you may not feel it, you may not believe it, you may not sense it. Maybe no one has told you, not even you to yourself. But this is how it is. You are a wise, spiritual being. Every human being is. In fact, there are no idiots at all, there are only wise, spiritual beings who pretend to be idiots. Who think they are idiots or would like to be idiots (it would serve them or suit them, for example). You arc a wise, spiritual being, full of essential knowledge and power, a very strong will, and unlimited energy. But someone who does stupid things, chooses them or tolerates them, like everyone else. Even the most "advanced," the most "spiritual," the most "enlightened" of people do this.

What is the difference? The sooner you realize that a situation is stupid and not love, and you choose to return to true respect, appreciation, and love for yourself and the other, the more conscious, spiritual, enlightened person you become. Freer, fuller, happier. And vice versa: the more conscious, spiritual, enlightened you are, the faster you realize which attitudes, choices, and situations are not love, but pure stupidity. This awareness is enough to think more, to reflect, to "search," to mobilize and move, to turn and do the best you can.

Perhaps you play the role of the victim? The unhappy, the suffering? Or the role of the "nice person," who sacrifices, who tolerates, who forgives, who endures, who stays and "loves"? Maybe you like it on some level? Maybe it suits you? Are you used to it? Is this what you have been taught? Is this what you have known? Do you derive self-worth from this, that you are "at least" someone, something useful, something good? Do you get crumbs of recognition and supposed appreciation? But is it good to draw external (and therefore unstable and fluid) self-worth, minimal appreciation, and almost no recognition from such a role that is unpleasant, causes pain, and perpetuates a negative situation? It is not an accusation, it is some food for thought: some general remarks and some more specific questions. We have all done it at some point; all people do it, to some degree. But to what extent, until when and why? For what reason? What alternative is there? Is there anything better than that? Is there anything else and what?

It is crucial, for a start, to unscramble yourself. To see that staying, accepting, or condoning a situation that does not contain love, appreciation, and respect, or is a situation of insincerity, oppression, or even violence, is stupidity and only stupidity, pure stupidity. Of the worst kind, actually: a stupidity that a wise, spiritual being, a conscious being does. A being of wisdom and love. Doing nothing about such a situation is nonsense. And a stupidity can always change.

What can you do about this situation you are experiencing? Can you do something and what? Can you react? Speak, express your thoughts and feelings? Walk away, escape, leave? Talk to friends, relatives? Is there anyone who can advise you or help you? Someone trusted? Do you have to contact the authorities, the police? In cases of violence, contacting the police is the solution. If it is your case, do it. Should you look for solutions online? Should you call specialized agencies? See a specialist counselor, psychologist, or psychotherapist? Try to improve things? What is the best solution for you? Can you help the other, others, and if so, how? Or is it not possible, is it a waste of effort and time, beyond your own power? No matter how hard you try, is it still the same thing and additional pain? Do you need to stay and continue to endure and, if so, until when and why? What are the alternatives? Think, reflect, connect with others, communicate and ask for help.

I am not able to know what is right for each case. It depends. What is absolute is that there is no need and it is not necessary to accept and tolerate forever anything that contains oppression and violence and not true respect, appreciation, and love. This is the essential, the true, the absolute. Everything else that may affect this all becomes highly relevant: relevant decisions, personal and special, that you have to think, weigh, dare, decide.

Whatever you choose, there is fear, the fear of change, but at the same time, whatever you choose, there is the light of hope. Light defeats darkness, if we choose it. You are already paying the highest price: you have stayed, more than you need and more than you want, in a situation that you do not deserve, that the other person does not deserve and that no one deserves. This is not spirituality and love. It is time to change your attitude, to adopt a behavior of true spirituality and true love.

Whatever you decide, you must recognize that whenever any conscious, spiritual being of wisdom and love accepts and compromises with something wrong, painful, or negative, then this choice is just stupid. One must recognize it as such and transcend it, seeking solutions and resources or improvement and change, in every possible and feasible way.

Forgiveness does not mean and is not "I tolerate," nor "I allow," nor "I accept," nor "I reenter," in this unpleasant, painful, or negative situation caused to you by another. It means recognizing stupidity as such, as non-love, and proceeding lightly and clearly, without weight, malice, resentment, bitterness, anger, fear, sadness, and revenge. You proceed by fully healing the wound, learning from it and improving yourself and your life. Spirituality and love do not tolerate and do not allow violence and oppression of any kind. They leave no space. They are not in the same space. They are incompatible. You cannot be in both at the same time. You have to choose.

Connect with who you are: a wise, spiritual being of unlimited love but also of unlimited wisdom and power. You have infinite and absolute worth, simply because you live, because you are human, and because you are yourself (no one else can be you; only you are you!). Appreciate and respect yourself; you were born with yourself and you live with yourself. Think, decide, and choose the best for yourself.

By choosing the best for you, you help others see their mistakes and do the same, recognize themselves as what they are: a wise, spiritual being, with moments and periods of stupidity, who tolerates and reconciles with situations of stupidity. They will do it. Sooner or later. Everyone has his/her own time. But yours is now. By choosing your "now moment," your next "now moment" and all the next "now moments" that you wish to be better, you help others, too. You encourage them to follow your example, to overcome these inferior, negative, or unpleasant situations. To improve them and change them, as much as possible. Or to leave, to make them a thing of the past and to walk again to the right and better – for them and for all – future.

TRANSCENDING DISAPPOINTMENT

The behavior of some people around me disappoints me.

It is natural and expected. And you have disappointed others in the past. And it will happen, most likely, in the future. At times, more or less, everyone disappoints everyone!

Each person acts according to the knowledge he/she has. People do not know. "One thing I know is that I know nothing," in all its glory and not in the good sense! They do not know: neither who they are, nor what they want, nor where they are moving to. They live without cause, meaning, and purpose, randomly and chaotically. They have not developed their talents, their intelligence, their wisdom, or their power. They are slaves of others, of the environment, of society, of the system, of their feelings and thoughts, of their habits and subconscious motives, of their "evil" self. Often, if not most of the time. A few, if not many. Unconscious and unconnected from self, others, nature, the whole. Isn't that enough to justify them, to understand them, to forgive them? It is in the human nature, it is part of us, and we are all part of it.

So just understand and forgive. Forgiveness comes only through true understanding. Everyone does what they can, based on what they know. And they usually know very little. And the worst is when they think they know a lot or even "everything." That's how we all are, that's how human beings are. The best thing we can do is to forgive. We forgive and try to correct our own perspective, our own way, our own behavior. Definitely, there are things we can always improve by increasing our knowledge, our knowledge on all levels.

Think about it, consider, and meditate on it. And confirm it:

"I release and forgive the person who disappointed me. Who hurt me, betrayed me, upset me. He/She did what he/she could, according to what he/she knew. He/She did what he/she knew, he/she did exactly what he/she knew. I release him/her fully and completely and I forgive him/her really and truly. In order to do that, I ask for the help and support of the higher intelligence and power of life and I let myself go to it completely, with confidence and security. I wish the best to this person, I forgive him/her, I release him/her and

Georgios Mylonas (Geom!)*

from now on I am attuned to increasingly better situations and attitudes. From now on, I increase the knowledge, appreciation, respect, and love I have for life, for myself, for others, and for the whole, and I connect with people who do the same more and more each time!"

THE PATH FROM UNHAPPINESS TO HAPPINESS

———————— ✸ ————————

I feel deep dissatisfaction and lack of any meaning and purpose in my life!

I am unhappy!

There has never been a human being who has found "happiness" in materialism. And there is no human being who has not experienced "happiness" through spirituality. This is expected and natural, for a very simple reason: the human being is a spiritual being. That is, it is a biological organism, a material body that has inner, existential, spiritual pursuits. Or a soul, a spirit, a consciousness in human form, embodied, manifested in matter. See it as you wish. A spiritual being, in any case.

A spiritual being can live in the world of matter but cannot find happiness in it alone. Through dull, plain, prosaic materialism. And this is the main philosophy, the way of perception and the life pattern of the system and, often, of the many. A spiritual being, however, can be happy only through his/her own essence, through his/her own nature – that is, through spirituality.

Happiness has many meanings: To find meaning and purpose, value and direction; to feel peace, security, trust; to experience fullness and freedom; to give and receive care and warmth; to connect genuinely and communicate truly; to find deeper satisfaction; to express your talents and potential and to feel loved and important; to help and offer; to enjoy life, the "now," the moments; to have health and love; to let others, your loved ones, do and experience the same. All of these compose what we generally and vaguely call "happiness" (no, happiness has nothing to do with the perfect families in the ads who buy everything and smile all the time!).

Matter is good, beautiful, and wonderful; we live in it and through it, but there is not a sufficient amount of "matter" nor its pleasures, which can give you any of the above.

We only reach happiness through spirituality, then, and that is by definition.

But what is "spirituality?" It is a general and vague term that can have many meanings: introspection and self-knowledge, self-improvement and personal development, meditation and spiritual practices, energy techniques and holistic healing, study and learning, esotericism and metaphysics, religion and philosophy, science and research, creation and art, holistic perception and a natural way of life, humanities and social studies work, offer and support, social and cultural action, action for fellow human beings and the environment. Anything that brings you into deeper contact with yourself but also with nature, with the universe, with the Whole. With the unknown, the greatest, the wonderful. With the higher, with the divine – no matter how we approach it, we perceive and understand it (or not). All of the above individually or in combinations are spiritual needs, qualities, aspects, and expressions of human beings. Spiritual. In matter but not of matter.

Many confuse spirituality with religion. Religion is a part and expression of human spirituality but it is not the only one. Many people think that spirituality is to be eccentric and isolated, to get lost in books, to dress strangely or to wear a chlamys, to meditate or to do yoga, to light candles, and to chant "Om." It may be all of these, but it is not just that!

Spirituality is the spiritual expression of human beings, which has many forms and aspects. Spirituality is anything that takes you beyond the narrow limits of matter and materialism. Anything that takes you beyond: "I live only to work, sleep and eat," "I consume and acquire more and more, in order to 'be', to exist, to have value," and "I am addicted: the source of my strength and happiness lies entirely on others, on relationships, money, external circumstances."

Spirituality is to be aware, to live awake and consciously, to try to see beyond the obvious and the apparent, to adopt different perspectives, and to try to see things more broadly, totally, and holistically. To be creative. To be simple, honest, direct, authentic, without many additional and unnecessary things. To have an inquiring, exploratory mind and spirit. To learn and to evolve. To wish for improvement, healing, and the good of all and work toward it every day. To see the connections and the unity of all. To become more and more the co-creator of your life and the master of yourself, choosing as much as possible what you think, feel, say, and do. To act wisely and consciously, instead of reacting, automatically and mechanically. To consciously choose the good, with all your beingness.

We are all spiritual beings, we all have inner, existential, creative needs, needs of self-knowledge and self-improvement, self-acceptance and self-realization, of personal development and personal evolution. We all have an innate transcendental tendency, a tendency to go "higher" or "beyond" mere matter and prosaic materialism. We are all spiritual beings but we are not all aware of it – we do not know it, and this is very important and makes all the difference in the world.

When you do not consciously know that you are a spiritual being, a spiritual existence, it is as if you live only from the plane and level of matter, of "what I can see is all that exists" and "things are how they appear to be." You live, believing that "material, external situations determine me completely and all my happiness depends on them," therefore, "only when I do … will I be well." You live through "I have, in order to be worthy," "I have, in order to be." Living only on the material plane, only materialistically, you live one-dimensionally, at a very primary level of life. Happiness is on a higher level. Happiness lies deeper.

If you want to find "happiness," all these important things that I have mentioned and which comprise happiness – meaning, value, purpose, direction, fullness, peace, joy – then turn toward what is essential. This is your essence. The essential is your essence and your essence is the only essential. Your "inner aspect." But also your "upper." Your "beyond." Your potential, what you have not expressed, created, and experienced, yet. Your inner, higher, true, authentic self, your spirit and your soul – many terms can be used, they are all important and wonderful and show something extra to this unknown and greater being that you really are. Turn toward this, toward the essential, with all your power, and do not leave it. Make it a priority, have it as your guide, and follow it at all costs and in every possible way. It is the path to happiness but it is also happiness itself.

EVERY EXPERIENCE IS A LESSON, BUT WHICH LESSON?

I experience various challenges and difficulties; is there any meaning, any deeper purpose in them?

My relationship with a person is negative and I wonder, why am I going through all this?

A great misfortune happened in my life. Was it really a misfortune or was there a reason it happened?

I have a health problem, what can it mean, is it a lesson?

This is probably the most important exercise you can do, on an inner, on a spiritual level. It is an exercise that contributes greatly to your personal development, gives new meaning and direction, truly illuminates your being, and fully enlightens your life.

According to the spiritual teachings, human life is a lesson, a lesson in the school of matter, a lesson in the school of the earth. Or rather, a series of lessons. By recognizing these inner or hidden lessons, realizing and assimilating them, we develop, grow, evolve. We become wiser and stronger. We stop making mistakes, we go with the flow, we follow the universal laws, we experience more positivity, positive situations. We come in greater contact with ourselves, with the universe, but also with the spiritual dimension of existence and the source of all.

Every experience, every situation, is a lesson, which aims to help us in our evolution and advancement, in our self-knowledge and enlightenment, in our union with all that is, our liberation, fulfillment, and theosis – the complete union with the Divine. Every experience contains a gift, a substance, a lesson. A knowledge and a power.

How do we take these lessons, how do we learn? Do we learn easily or with difficulty? At a fast or slow pace? Is it a painless or a painful process? Are we good students? Or are we repeating some lessons? Life and the universe, existence, will offer us the lesson, again and again, until we receive it and fully understand it. It is something we, ourselves desire, on a spiritual level, at the level of the soul. Quite simply, we strongly and deeply desire to live, to experience, to learn, to become. To develop our consciousness. And this can only be done through life, only through the world and the universe, through matter, that is, through earthly experiences and human experiences.

What do the situations you live in mean? What do the things that happen and that you experience mean? Do they mean something?

If one is absolutely sure that they don't mean anything, that everything is coincidental, that situations and experiences do not have a deeper or inner meaning and purpose, then this exercise does not interest him/her. But if one is open to the fact that there is probably some meaning, some substance, some lesson, then this exercise can prove to be extremely helpful and beneficial, even transformative or therapeutic. Let's start, then!

EXERCISE: WHAT CAN YOU LEARN FROM THIS?

What can you learn from each situation? To put it in another way: if you were to learn something, what would it be?

Take a piece of paper and write on it, as a title, the issue that concerns you. A difficulty or a situation. Any topic that concerns you intensely: health, family, relationships, love, abundance, work, emotions, spirituality, life purpose.

Write the issue on the paper. You can write it in general, as a field of life, for example: abundance, work, family, health and so on. Or more specifically, for example: a problem with ..., a lack of ..., difficulty with ..., a specific health issue (specify exactly) or specific problem with a person (specify the individual). That is, you can write the title in a nutshell or in more detail.

Below, write: "What can I learn:"

Underline everything to make it look like a title and then leave the page blank below, so that you can think and write down your answers there. Write whatever comes to mind. Relax, take your time, and do not rush. Take a few deep breaths, slowly and steadily, calmly. Relax more and leave your mind empty and free. Whatever comes to mind, observe it and write it down. Pause and think. Do it calmly, slowly, internally, like a meditation. Write, without judging, freely, spontaneously.

Here are three examples.

Health Issue (you can make it specific)
What can I learn:

I can learn what it is like/what it means to be sick.
I can learn the value of health.
I can learn to be strong.
I can learn to listen to my body.

I can learn to take care of my body.
I can learn to express my feelings.
I can learn to rest.
I can learn that I can be healed.
I can learn to let others take care of me.
I can learn to strengthen my energy.
I can learn what is good for me and what is not.
I can learn to trust, to look for solutions, to endure, to be patient.
…

Relationship Issue (you can make it specific)
What can I learn:

I can learn to be my best self.
I can learn to understand, to forgive.
I can learn to live together, to join hands.
I can learn to be patient, to make concessions, to look for solutions, to trust.
I can learn to communicate.
I can learn to get to know the other person better.
I can learn to get to know myself more.
I can learn what a lack of love and care is like.
I can learn love and care.
I can learn to set boundaries.
I can learn to manage my emotions.
I can learn to improve.
…

Abundance Issue/Work Issue (you can make it specific)
What I learn:

I can learn to manage money.
I can learn to live with a little money.
I can learn to make more money.
I can learn how to be creative.
I can learn what it is like to work somewhere I do not like.
I can learn to claim.
I can learn to find solutions, to be patient, to adapt, to cooperate.
I can learn myself.
I can learn to appreciate myself.
I can learn to be creative.
I can learn to become strong.
I can learn to have self-esteem, self-confidence.
I can learn what it is like not to have respect and appreciation.
I can learn to give and receive respect and appreciation.

…

You can write positive things, things that you learn and receive, but also negative things (essentially, they have a positive effect). For example, in a relationship where you are belittled and rejected, you can learn what it is like to be rejected, this unpleasant experience, and the thoughts and feelings associated with it. And, at the same time, you can learn that you do not deserve something like that or that you would like something else to happen to you (to be accepted and appreciated). You can learn to tolerate, to be patient but you can also learn to claim, to become stronger, to choose the change, to leave, to move forward, to change. You can learn about yourself and your boundaries, what is fair/just/right and what is not, the balance and the imbalance, the goodness or lack of it, the serenity or the opposite, the love or the fear. You can learn the pleasant and the unpleasant, what exactly you do not like and what exactly you would like.

Write freely, take your time, do not rush.

When you realize what exactly you can learn from each situation, especially when it is undesirable and unpleasant, you can realize the next stage: "Fine, I have learned this! I have learned it well! I have really learned it, I have experienced it well! Thank you very much! I will go somewhere else now, I will move on, I will go further, to the next level, to the next stage!"

When you have really realized what you can learn from each situation, when you truly recognize and appreciate it, then it really does happen, you can go further, to other lessons, new, more enjoyable than before. It is the journey of life in its easiest, most favorable and enjoyable version!

NON-ATTACHMENT

> *How can I be happier? Calmer, happier in my daily life? I feel trapped in many situations. I feel that I depend on many factors.*

You need to know a vital condition of spirituality. To know it, recognize it, and then practice on it. To have it, as much as possible, in your mind and bring, as often as possible, your attention to it. To adopt it and make it your own, your nature.

This term is "non-attachment."

Non-attachment is the beginning, the basis, and the framework, the necessary condition, and the essential assurance of every true happiness. Of freedom, fulfillment, and happiness.

It is really valid and unquestionably experienced: Non-attachment equals freedom, equals fulfillment, equals happiness.

On the other hand, we find attachment: dependence on … (this could be any possible element). Attachment is the source of all mental pain but also the affirmation of personal misery.

Non-attachment is a term, a concept, a principle that requires a mental and spiritual process, analysis, elaboration, and understanding, it needs awareness and daily meditation. It is a supreme principle, a direction of daily conscious life.

Ask yourself: "Where/What am I attached to and why? What would non-attachment be in this situation?"

Every pain and misery is a possible attachment – or it is partly an attachment. Every obstacle, every blockage, every darkness, every negative element springs from or is related to attachment. Material, energetic, emotional, or mental attachment. Either combinations of those levels, or all of them together.

Recognizing, becoming aware of the attachment is as much as half the healing; it is a release.

Recognizing the attachment, becoming aware of the obsession, the dependence, the blockage, is the existential, conscious, and energetic opening to non-attachment as well as to the existential, conscious, and energetic goods that non-attachment contains, which it so abundantly, easily, and pleasantly carries within it.

It is good to have preferences, instead of attachments. It makes a huge difference, emotionally and mentally, a huge spiritual and energy difference.

"I have preferences, not attachments." Incorporate this into your life, make it your mantra, keep it in mind, and whisper it whenever you need it. "I have preferences, not attachments."

"I prefer" means "I choose." That is, "I set my freedom and consciousness in motion." I prefer, I choose, I mobilize my awareness, psyche, intellect, and spirituality. I express them, I put them in motion and action. On the other hand, attachment has no movement, no action, no choice, no freedom, no awareness. Attachment has shackles, immobilization, a lack of freedom, restraint, blocking, and sticking to something specific, which usually creates conflict, anger, sadness, and pain within us.

So I have preferences. I prefer. I prefer this, that, then, there, this way. I prefer to be like this, I prefer to have these, I prefer to experience this, I prefer to think like this, to feel this. I prefer to relate in that way and to these people. I prefer to learn these, to see these, to hear these, to act and react in this way…

Georgios Mylonas (Geom!*)

I prefer, I prefer, I prefer: these and those, this way or another, now and here and in this form. I choose and prefer without dependence, I prefer and choose without attachment. I prefer and choose with love, I prefer and choose with wisdom, I prefer and choose with awareness. Consciously, responsibly, spiritually, creatively, peacefully, harmoniously. I release constantly, I release and I do not cling to anything, I do not get attached. I do not stop, I do not stagnate and, therefore, I do not sink. After all, flow means life and life means flow.

Our whole life is a path from the myriad semi-conscious, unconscious, and subconscious attachments (negative habits, shackles, blockages, obstacles, and dependencies) to the specifically conscious choice and the sustained conscious preference. The preference of choice, the preference of non-attachment. The choice and preference of absolute freedom, of supreme fulfillment, and of the deep and essential bliss that we deserve and in fact are.

Non-attachment for everyone and non-attachment for everything, then. Non-attachment to everyone and non-attachment to everything!

Consciously, with Love!

With Love, Consciously!

DILEMMAS AND DECISIONS

--- ✸ ---

> *I have a dilemma and I have to make an important decision. How do I know which is the right, best choice?*

A body is made up of countless cells. Imagine a tiny cell inside a body. So is a human being; so are you. A cell in the great body of Life, a cell in the infinite body of Existence. A universal and important cell, a truly wonderful and beautiful cell!

How can a cell make the best decision, the right decision for any issue, for anything? The more connected and aware it is of itself, its environment, and the whole body of which it is a part, the better the decision. The better the decision for itself, and for the total, for the Whole. After all, the best for the cell is the best for the body and the best for the body is the best for the cell. They are interconnected, due to their unity, existential and absolute. The best for you is the best for the Whole and the best for the Whole is the best for you.

Since it has free will, the cell has two options: either to isolate itself and feel disconnected and out of tune with the body, which has negative consequences, or to open up and connect with the larger body to which it belongs, to connect and to receive its great wisdom and power. This is the best possible choice and the only one that assures every possible good.

So the more you come in contact with yourself and the Whole, the more open and receptive, connected and attuned you are to the wisdom and power that exists within you and within the greater Whole, the closer to the wisdom and power of Life and Existence you are, the more correct are the decisions you make and the better the choices. The more "present" you are in your cell and in the Whole. The more aware you are. The more conscious you are.

But how does this happen? Is the intention enough?

The intention, to think that this is indeed something good for you and, in fact, the best for you, is important. To consider it more deeply, to think about it more, to make a decision, to focus on it, is even more important. But how do you focus on that? How do you focus more on being "present," conscious, aware? How do you focus more on connecting with your inner and outer world, on tuning in to a bigger, higher, deeper, wider field of wisdom, power, and potential?

There are various methods and people see a variety of positive results with them. Dare, experiment, practice, and devote time and energy to these methods. They are tools that help you achieve exactly what you want, what you consider best for you. Among these tools, among these methods, are meditation and visualization, introspection and self-observation, deep relaxation, conscious, focused thinking and the use of positive words/speech, holistic therapy methods, natural lifestyle and contact with nature, energy therapies, self-knowledge and psychotherapy processes, methods of self-improvement and personal development, prayer and spiritual study, love and offering to the others.

Any inner, energy, or spiritual work is essentially a tool and a path to reach this connection with your inner world and with the Whole, as consciously as possible, as much as possible. To become more "present," more awakened, more conscious, more aware, inside you and inside Life and Existence.

If you do any of the above, you are on the right track! Continue with faith and optimism, with patience and love. You become a more open and receptive human being, more serene and pure, while you become more and more connected with your own wisdom and power and with the larger body of Life and Existence. The decisions you will make, the choices you will make will be better and better, more and more correct, for you and for the Whole. So feel the depth of this belief. Feel it in your cells. In all your cells.

"I am in touch with myself, with my true, authentic, complete, beloved self. With the source of wisdom and power within me. With Life itself, Existence, and the Whole. In harmony with everything, in connection with everything, in tune with everything. Life, Existence, and the Whole love and support me completely, just as their beloved child and all of them want the best for me. So do I, and I recognize, appreciate, respect, and love Life, Existence, and the Whole and I desire only the best for all and for everything. I open, experience and practice the maximum breadth, height, and depth of my wisdom, love, and power, I am a strong, responsible, awakened, and conscious being and I know that all my decisions and choices are the best possible and constantly better! I am grateful for that and, from the bottom of my soul, thank you!"

STEPS OF AWARENESS

— ✳ —

How can I know if what I do in my daily life is good? That is, if it is for good? From good and for the good? If it is positive, if it actually helps me and others evolve? If it is in alignment with the higher, the spiritual element, with true love and wisdom?

There is a very important exercise that you can do for your spiritual growth. It is called "Steps of Awareness." It is about being more conscious, by observing and studying your motivations for everything you are doing.

Examine your motives… the reason why you do everything.

Where does your every thought, word, feeling come from? Every choice, deed, and action? What is its purpose, how does it affect you, what does it offer, what does it mean? Examine often – daily – your motives, causes, the source.

But also the purpose, the effect, the potential impact. As much as possible, as much as you can. After your every action. Even better – ideally – before your every action, before your every expression and deed. Pause and observe, stop every now and then, whenever necessary, and ask yourself. Get into a state of awareness, wake up, awaken yourself, be present, become conscious.

"What was the cause, the source, the motive, for what I did? For what I thought, I said and I chose? And what is the motive and the source, what is the cause, for what I think and wish to choose, express, say, and do in the now and in the future? Do they have a meaning, a substance? Do they have a purpose and what is it?"

Make it an exercise and a practice. A habit and a way of life, an attitude and a point of view, consciously and with awareness. Make it consciousness and awareness.

Bringing your awareness, your consciousness, through simple observation, self-observation, and introspection, to everything you think, feel, choose, do and express, that is, in every action and deed, you change, you transform, you transmute yourself. You become a being of increased consciousness, a more conscious being.

Gradually, the deeds and actions that you generate, that you manifest and express, come more in alignment with who you really are. With your true self, with your essence.

They are no longer random, asynchronous, or peripheral, they become essential. Your actions and deeds gain higher power and carry deeper wisdom, as they spring more and more from a better, brighter spot of yours, more pure, serene, harmonious, beautiful, and true.

When the source, the cause, the motive is pure, bright, good, positive, serene, harmonious, beautiful, and true, then the purpose, the meaning, the effect is exactly the same. Energy, action itself, cannot be something else, something different.

This change, the transformation, the transmutation is the most important process of human life, the most essential for human existence and the being of humans. It is a process, a route, a course, with many names. Self-knowledge, self-improvement, self-realization. Empowerment, healing, happiness. Development, evolution, ascension. It is none other than the process, the path, the course of Enlightenment. And all the steps toward it are steps of consciousness, steps of awareness.

Therefore, pause, think, ask yourself, more and more. Examine your motives, the reason you do everything.

You take conscious steps, steps of awareness. Bright, illuminated... these are the steps of enlightenment!

THE COMMON SECRET IS THE SECRET ELEMENT

We often complain about the situations and quality of life, about our finances, our work, our health status, and our relationships with others. And rightly so! Because we deserve the best, we deserve all the good things and can acquire them, experience them, enjoy them. The more we put our efforts into them, the more we work toward them, the more we progress, learn, grow, evolve. Our journey into the world of matter is our journey to our own soul. A journey outward, as much as a journey inward.

All the experiences of our lives are valuable lessons that make us what we will become, what we are constantly becoming, what we really are: a complete, full, bright, and enlightened, calm and peaceful, conscious and wise, free and ecstatic being. This is and this will be done, this is being done constantly, through everything that we perceive, process, learn, recognize, and realize.

There is a very good exercise you can do, an inner exercise, an exercise of consciousness – after all, aren't they all like that?

What do all those that find themselves in the same situation have in common? In a similar field or level? Although there are no kinds or categories of people, because every person is special, distinct and unique, precious and sacred, let's suppose, for the sake of this exercise, that there are some general "categories." Some common features, properties, characteristics. Some common energy elements.

For example, those who experience abundance, great abundance. Those who have good relationships. Those who experience a great love. Those who are successful in some field. Those who are creative, who have inspiration. Those who have discovered something important. Those who are healthier. Those who were cured of a difficult disease. Those who overcame a great loss or a tragic event. Those who have healed a great mental trauma. Those who awoke, were enlightened, experienced divine love and bliss, discovered the divine element. Those who have developed gifts or talents. Those who are magnetic, attractive, beloved. Those who make a difference in any field. Those who do good, who contribute, who help, who heal, who teach, who care, who protect, who guide.

Focus on a "category" that interests you.

What do people who "belong" to this "category" have in common? Those who experience a similar situation, a specific characteristic, a quality or property, or have a specific level or type of life? Do they have anything in common? In other words: If they had something in common, what would it be?

Make a list. Sit down, relax, and then concentrate, think and write.

For example: What do those who experience abundance, great abundance, positive flow, prosperity, comfort, and ease in their finances and material level have in common?

Some negative elements may come to your mind, in relation to those who experience great abundance. They are not the ideal example, the standard, so leave those and focus on people you admire and who have plenty of abundance. People who have succeeded through their value, through their work. Like people who use their abundance positively, for good. Are there such people? Who are they? Did you bring them to your mind? Nice. What do they have in common? Relax, think calmly, and reflect – you will come up with various nice thoughts and enlightening ideas.

And finally, think, what is their "common energy?" Close your eyes and ask to acquire it, to adopt it, to receive it, and to experience it yourself. Stay in this thought for a while and meditate on this energy, feel it. The energy of those who experience abundance, great abundance, positive flow, prosperity, comfort, and ease in their finances and material level.

Do the same for all "categories."

Those who overcame some serious health issue, some great loss, some significant difficulty. What do they have in common? It may be good luck, to have good luck on their side. Write it. They may have positive energy, positive emotional state, strength. Write it. They may have external help and support, a good, positive, supportive environment. Write it. What else? Do they have anything else? Inner characteristics, qualities, properties? Choices, emotions, a way of thinking and acting? Write everything, many things will come to your mind. Do not rush.

And finally, what is their "common energy?" Close your eyes and ask to acquire it, to adopt it, to receive it and to experience it yourself. Stay in this thought for a while and meditate on this energy, feel it. The energy of those who overcame some serious health issue, some great loss, some significant difficulty.

What do those who experience beautiful, good, quality, deep, true, bright, beloved relationships have in common? Relationships of great love and relationships of great romance? Do you know such people? Do some people come to your mind? Sure, they too have challenges and issues and their life or relationship is not a fixed, straight line; it has "ups and downs," good and bad, pleasant and unpleasant, positive and negative moments. But they have something you admire and desire. What element is this? Love, affection, communication, trust, joy, duration, care, understanding, matching, chemistry? Something else? Fine, now think of the common element that everyone who experiences what you admire and desire has. What is this? Good luck, fate, karma, environment, character? All these together? Something else? Do they have common elements in their character, in the way of perception and thinking, common talents, abilities, qualities, virtues? Think and write.

And finally, what is their "common energy"? Close your eyes and ask to acquire it, to adopt it, to receive it, and to experience it yourself. Stay in this thought for a while and meditate on this energy, feel it. The energy of those who experience beautiful, good, quality, deep, true, bright, beloved relationships.

After this exercise, it is easier to integrate the specific energies in your life and in yourself. The virtues, abilities, properties, and qualities. Adaptability, organizational capacity, good management, discernment, patience, perseverance, positivity, focus, determination, diligence, discipline, industriousness, mobility, ingenuity, imagination, activism, dynamism, energy, fearlessness, boldness, inspiration, ability to do research, insight, continuous learning, ability to overcome the past, goals, dreams, a change of beliefs, readjustment, self-confidence, endurance, sensitivity, friendliness, serenity, kindness, forgiveness, a good aura, an open mind, an open heart, body care, quality of life, good feelings, balance, grounding, spirituality, alternative ways of thinking, awareness and so much more, which are probably shared by those who experience something good, beautiful and true!

So think about it. All those who experience something good, beautiful, and true, that you admire and desire – health, strength, peace, abundance, prosperity, love, transcendence, evolution – have a "secret." Something they share, something that connects them, a common element. Or rather more elements. Internal and external elements, spiritual and material. But also an energy, a specific energy, the energy of what they experience. Their common secret is their secret element. And yes, if we want it, it applies to all of us, we can all perceive and recognize it, choose and adopt it and, finally, experience and live it. And then, quite simply, our common secret will be our secret element!

THE HIDDEN INTELLIGENCE OF EXISTENCE

"We and the World, Part 1: Mirror, mirror, who is the smartest, the most intelligent, and the wisest, in the whole world?"

Do you know that the universe is alive, conscious, and intelligent? Not like us humans. Much more and in a different way. It is infinitely alive, conscious, and intelligent. Despite the rumors, vitality, consciousness, and intelligence are not exclusively human privileges or gifts. Even though this is how it seems. They are parts, qualities, expressions, of something bigger than the human being, something much bigger, equally wonderful, alive and intelligent, if not even more.

Usually, we, human beings believe, having cut off and convinced ourselves of this, that we are "above" what lies "around" us, we are "higher" than what is found "outside."

More intelligent than our environment. Than life, nature, the universe, existence, and reality, of which we are a very small part and a relatively recent creation. But such a thing is only an illusion, a pure delusion.

How could something non-intelligent, non-living ever create something alive and intelligent? It is like saying that a painting, no matter how exquisite, beautiful, and "intelligent" it is, is superior to the artist, to its creator. The artist already contains the painting, all its wisdom and beauty, while the opposite is not true, the painting does not contain the whole of the artist. The painting is a small part of the artist, a single expression of him/her, while the artist is much bigger and transcendental in relation to his/her creation.

This in no way diminishes the unique value, vitality, intelligence, and beauty of the creation. We, human beings, however, often tend to underestimate. Ourselves, others, and the Whole. The environment, existence, and reality in which we live. The very life given to us. We consider them scenes of our daily lives, lifeless, neutral, random, chaotic. In some cases, even hostile. We think that we stand out from the scene, as the only conscious or intelligent being. We cannot imagine, nor can we conceive, how much consciousness, vitality, intelligence, and wisdom are required to create every molecule of existence. To create us even more so, a miracle of nature, an art of maximum value and beauty. A double mirror that perceives and observes the inside and the outside.

As an exercise, you can begin to see and perceive your environment as intelligent. The universe and the world, nature and life, existence, and reality. As supremely intelligent, supremely conscious, and supremely alive. Not in the human way alone. In a bigger, higher, more transcendental way. More universal and more cosmic. In an unknown way. Begin to perceive life as infinitely conscious, infinitely wise, infinitely intelligent, infinitely alive, in an unknown, transcendental, universal, cosmic way. Do the same for the environment and the world, nature and the universe. For the whole of existence.

When you really do this, when you start doing it, as soon as you dare to do it (it takes courage to recognize the – unknown until recently – intelligence), amazing things happen. Your life is no longer isolated or unconnected. It is not accidental or chaotic. Neither closed nor lonely. Everything, anything, the whole universe, and the totality of existence is now with you. Infinitely intelligent, absolutely conscious, supremely alive.

"More and more, I recognize and realize the unlimited and supreme wisdom-intelligence, which surrounds me and is everywhere! More and more, I recognize and realize the infinite and absolute intelligence-wisdom of life, the universe and the whole of existence!"

THE IDEAL RELATIONSHIP WITH LIFE AND THE WHOLE

"We and the World, Part 2: A Relationship, But What Relationship?"

Have you ever wondered: What is your relationship with the universe? With what is "outside" or "around" of you, with the environment in which you live? The world, nature, animals, plants, stones, water, air, sun, planets, and stars? With humanity as a whole? With life itself? With the universe, existence, the Whole?

Do you have a relationship? What kind of relationship? No relationship? A cold relationship, a distant one? Unconscious, non-personal? Could it be better? Could it get stronger? What would be the perfect, ideal relationship?

Imagine a human being who has the ideal relationship with what is "around" and "outside" of him/her. With everything and anything. With existence and with life. With the universe and with the world. Imagine this person having a close, very personal relationship with everything that exists. Direct, deep, substantial. Full of respect, appreciation, recognition, acceptance. A relationship of love, pure love, true love, deep love, total love. With proper communication, trust, and absolute acceptance. This person has and enjoys the ideal and the most perfect relationship of supreme love, supreme communication, and supreme trust with the universe, in which he/she lives, moves and breathes, with existence and with the very power of life.

This person does everything for the universe, for existence, for the Whole. And the Whole, existence, the universe, does everything for him/her. They talk and listen to each other, care for, support, and strongly desire each other's good and only that. There is a quality relationship of reciprocity, understanding, and honesty. There is great, maximum admiration, great, maximum commitment, and great, maximum appreciation. Easily and constantly, this human being sees and recognizes himself/herself everywhere in the universe and everything is an extension of him/her, aspects of his/her beingness. They are all important, sacred, and beloved.

Such a reciprocal, strong, and deep relationship with the Whole, a relationship of respect, love, trust, and appreciation, is absolutely possible and feasible for you to create, as well. With the environment, with the power of life, with the universe, with the world, with existence, with everything and anything. With nature, with the earth, and with humanity. A relationship with open, true communication and with continuous, substantial sharing, mutual help and support, an absolutely favorable, positive, evolutionary – for you and for all – relationship.

Imagine it as a very good relationship between a parent and a child. Or like a very good friendship. Or even as a very good romantic relationship. See the big universe as your real family. Existence, everything that exists, the Whole, like your best friend. Life or the whole world, like your loved one, like your partner. Like in absolute love, in which your "other half" (or your "other one," more correctly), lifts you up, elevates you, makes you fly and feel heavenly, helps you experience everyday life and the "now," with so much joy and power!

When you are friendly with the universe, it treats you the same way. When you are full of love, respect, and appreciation for life, for existence, it perceives you in exactly the same way. With so much acceptance, trust, care, and support. You open, you connect, you communicate with the greater Being and the greater Being opens, connects, communicates with you. When you are conscious of the universe, the universe is also conscious of you. When you are conscious of the Whole, the Whole is also conscious of you. When you are conscious of life, life is also conscious of you. So simple, so true. So equal and fair. Nothing less and everything more.

And the separation between the "outside" and the "inside" and vice versa is increasingly no longer valid. As in an ideal relationship. You become a single Whole, a complete One, in which life, love, and everything beautiful, good, and true flows naturally, freely, and abundantly.

Begin such a relationship today, so positive, so ideal! So conscious and of such a high quality! The "outside," the "other side," is waiting for you and it wants it too, it is ready. It has always been waiting for you, since it created you with such intelligence. If you are already in this relationship, you know how exquisite and important it is. Enjoy it to the fullest!

"I create and experience the ideal relationship of supreme love and perfect trust with the universe! With life, with existence, with the Whole. A relationship of true respect, recognition, and appreciation. Only understanding, acceptance, care, flow, and all good things exist among us. We are in perfect communication, we walk consciously together and we are continuously and always One!"

PICTURES OF VIOLENCE, ACTS OF LOVE

---------------- ✳ ----------------

Some thoughts, prompted by the images circulating on the Internet about the war and the refugees.

The images that are spread everywhere are extremely harsh and cause pain. It is almost impossible to avoid them and you are not supposed to, anyway. They are images of real events happening in the common reality we live in. It is important for someone to see them, as they are a fact and an expression of the misery and cruelty that exists. But they can be a powerful call for us to become even more conscious, even more human.

Only an object, a thing, has the right to say, "This is how things are, this is the reality," and to remain there unperturbed, shut in itself, as a thing, as an object.

Only a plant has the right to say, "I cannot do anything, I am rooted, immobile."

Only an animal has the right to say, "It does not touch me, therefore it does not concern me," or "Your death is my life."

A human being has the right and obligation to think, to reflect, to process: "What is happening out there?" "Why are things like this?" "What can I do?" "It concerns me completely," and "Your life, my life."

It does not matter if it is a specific war, a specific disaster, this tragedy, or something else. In the past it was something else and in the future it will be something different. There is always something out there that can be completely unpleasant, negative, bad, and tragic. It is not just a matter of what is happening – yes, we need to know what is going on, what is there, and explore the possible reasons on many levels. But still this is not enough. The issue is not just what happens, whether we know it and what the obvious or hidden causes are, but how we handle it.

How do we deal with everything that happens? If we say, "This is the harsh reality," "It does not concern me" or "I can do nothing," we fall into the state of the animal-plant-thing and move away from what we are: humane, conscious, spiritual beings. And yet this is who we are: "There is more to it than meets the eye."

It is natural and human to be filled with guilt and remorse when there is so much misery around. It shows that we are conscious, spiritual beings who perceive and process the world mentally and emotionally. It is natural to be filled with fear and dread, or sadness and frustration, or anger, even hatred. Everything shows that we are conscious beings, not just animals, plants, or things (pure unconscious matter, if any).

It is natural and human to be filled with these emotions, but it is important not to dwell on them. What can I help with and how? Spirituality and happiness, happiness and spirituality, are the same thing: it is the recognition and realization of the great power or will we have within us. Of the great wisdom or intelligence and of the great love or kindness. It is the development of our love-wisdom-power. Their recognition, realization, expression, and manifestation. Then you become a conscious, spiritual, happy (or complete, if you wish) person.

These are ideally found in Offering. To offer somewhere, in some way, to a single person, to reduce pain and increase joy, is the ideal action: the ideal love you can express, the ideal power you can express. The ideal wisdom you can express. So, offering is, the best (with love), the strongest and wisest thing you can do, in any situation and always. It contains wisdom, love, and power in their golden ratio. That is why the offering is an essential and vital part of all religions, but also of any other esoteric or spiritual system and teaching. It is our best, wisest, strongest (yes, it needs power to offer), superior side.

"Things happen" only to things. They are simple receivers, objects. A human being is substantial, and he/she has the ability to be a substantial being, a being of substance. And as conscious – or spiritual – beings we process, select, act, and influence what is outside of us; we shape it. From minimally and little, to a greater degree, directly and indirectly, individually and collectively. In many ways and on many levels. From the moment we experience the situations, from the most beautiful and pleasant to the most unpleasant and sad, we are human beings and as such we have the right but also the obligation to live.

CAN YOU OFFER TO THE WHOLE OF HUMANITY?

How can I offer and help more? There is great misery and pain in the world, poverty, inequality, lack of freedom, diseases, fear, conflicts, and war. I think about them often and sometimes I cannot stand it, I despair. I feel that I am not following the purpose of my life as much as I could – that is, I could do a lot in order to help, but I do not. I feel a bit lost and I really want to give and offer.

What you think shows that you are on the right track, as long as you do not overlook the other side, the positive, good, and beautiful side, which really exists on Earth. What you think shows that you are a compassionate, benevolent being, of higher sensitivity and, therefore, intelligent, awakened, conscious, aware, full of love and wisdom but also strength!

Concerning what you can do: Can you help a single person? Not many. One, only one person? That would be enough to be able to say on a spiritual level, "Yes, my life is complete, it is perfect, it is worth it, it has meaning, substance, and purpose." It is enough to make you feel, "Yes, I am grateful to be alive, I am grateful to be me, I am grateful to be me, now, here."

To a single person. To say something good and nice, to encourage and empower, to ease the pain, to give hope and support. What does this person need? Material goods, food, a house? Support, encouragement, consolation, healing, guidance, a smile, a caress, a hug? Honesty, appreciation, respect, communication? Care, friendship, love? What does that person need? Something material, something spiritual? Can you help him/her in one of the above and in what, at least, as much as you can?

One person, this person that you have near you, this person that is in front of you. He/she may be near you and in front of you in some other way, for example, through TV or through someone talking to you about that person. It is in front of you in any way, it is in front of your perception, your consciousness.

Can you help, and how? You can contribute in so many ways: act, communicate, show practical interest, care; support materially, offer money or goods; show appreciation, respect, and love, become a friend, hug; pray and meditate for his/her good, send positive thinking and energy; ask, learn, guide and connect the person with someone else or a group that knows more, that can offer or do what the person needs. There are so many things that you can do.

One person and then another person and then another person. You may help and offer to whoever is in front of you, close to you. In every way, in any way. Helping one person might be the same as if you reach out to help the whole of humanity. No, it is not a joke. There are people who have helped the whole of humanity, to a certain extent, to their own, to the extent that was their part. They did it in various ways. One molecule of help is enough and this much is needed from you.

Those who helped the whole of humanity did not start with the whole. They did not start with the whole of humanity – that would be an impossible task. They started with themselves and their neighbor, just him/her. Then the offer, the care, the knowledge, the idea, the healing, the love, the creation, their work, was simply channeled and transmitted, flared and imparted, either gradually or rapidly, in every direction, everywhere.

It does not matter how exactly this will be done in your case. It will happen. What matters is the human being, the person in front of you. Can you help and how? Do not go further; it is not necessary.

Remember: Everything you need is inside you. Constantly. And everything you need to do, every time, is in front of you. Always.

OFFER TO OUR EARTH

--- ✻ ---

> *How can I offer more, help the Earth and the whole*
> *energetically?*

Apart from the action and deeds, which are, of course, absolutely important and valuable, we can give, send our positive energy, our focused and strong healing thought, to the Earth, to our planet. Our energy, emotions, and thoughts act and affect on another, non-visible, deeper level, affecting not only us and the collective unconscious of humanity, but also the aura, the energy of the Earth and, therefore, of all beings.

Although they are not directly visible, our thoughts and feelings are not only experienced and exist, but are emitted and transmitted, recorded, and influenced, while we may say that they even have an autonomous existence from their owner, from their creator. By creating and keeping in our minds superior and good, positive and healing images, thoughts, and feelings, as much as we can and as often as we can, we contribute in a deeper and inner way to the good, the general or higher good. The good of the planet, the good of all.

Read the following text, very slowly and calmly, feel the words. It is something between a meditation and an invocation, it is like a prayer and a positive statement together. Do it meditatively, internally, emphasizing words and concepts with images in your mind and with superior, beautiful emotions such as love, peace, and joy. In addition, take three deep breaths at the beginning and three more at the end of the process. Slowly and deeply. Repeat the text two more times, three in total. Always slowly, calmly, and meditatively. Open, sensitize yourself, observe: how do you feel?

Do not have any doubts. You have offered essentially, you have added a very important element of positivity and healing to the Whole.

"We send Love to Earth, Light to Earth, Love and Light to Earth…

I send Love to Earth, Light to Earth, Love and Light to Earth…

More Light and more Love to Earth…

Greater Light and greater Love to Earth…

Higher Light and higher Love to Earth…

Love, Light, Love and Light, today and every day, now and constantly, to Earth…

I send the pure, warm, vital energy of Light and the pure, bright, healing energy of Love…

The Light of Love and the Love of Light, now, all over the Earth…

Supremely beloved Earth, supremely bright Earth!

Infinitely, absolutely and perfectly bright and perfectly, absolutely and infinitely beloved!

Let all the problems and wounds be healed, let them be healed deeply, completely, truly. The healing is happening, it is happening now…

Let us find the answers, directions, and solutions to all problems – true, superior, and wise. The answers, directions, and solutions are found, validated, and implemented now – truly, supremely, and wisely.

Let all situations be illuminated, with pure vital light, the perfect light of life and the true spirit. Let the minds and hearts, souls and bodies of all people and all creatures be enlightened. This enlightenment is activated and is happening now…

Let a new, higher, good, beautiful, true, and positive reality be created for everyone. It is created and experienced by everyone now…

Health, Peace, Serenity, Joy, Abundance, Prosperity, Strength, Wisdom, Harmony, Vitality, Awareness, Unity, Freedom, Fullness, Happiness, Gratitude, and All the Good Things! To Earth, to all humans and all creatures.

I turn, direct and focus my mind, energy, psyche, spirit, and my whole being to this. To the complete healing and perfect enlightenment of the Earth, of all humans and all creatures.

Here and now and constantly: I feel, I visualize, I declare and I confirm the complete healing and the perfect enlightenment of the Earth, of all people and of all creatures.

Light-Love-Life, Light-Love-Life, Light-Love-Life! To Earth, to all humans and all creatures.

It will be done, it is done now, it has already been done!

With infinite gratitude, thank you!"

COLLECTIVE KARMA

─────────────── ✻ ───────────────

In cases of general misery and economic collapse, such as the one we are experiencing in our country, what is the cause, on a spiritual level? The collective consciousness?

For all the issues and situations in the world, there are countless causes, on many levels. Individual, collective, social, economic, global, etc. The interests of the few, those who pull the worldwide strings. Those who have the global wealth and the control in their hands, the elite. In spiritual terms, those who move based only on their ego, only on interest and selfishness, on their lower self. Some call them "the dark ones" or "the power of evil." One can find many factors and causes for the various problems of humanity, and name them in even more ways.

Here, we will talk more about the internal, spiritual causes of a situation. Everything a person experiences, internally or spiritually, is a result of karma. The law of karma or, in other words, the law of cause-effect: any action has a reaction, every phenomenon has a cause and every phenomenon creates something else. "You reap what you sow." It is a universal, global, widespread spiritual law that includes the laws of nature. To be precise, the laws of nature are karma in its physical dimension, in its material level.

Right choices create good or positive karma, while wrong choices create bad or negative karma. Positive karma is pleasant and negative karma is unpleasant. To put it another way, negative choices, of all kinds, create negative effects and vice versa, good choices create positive results, positive situations.

But what is a "right" or "good" choice? It is an act driven by the highest energy and power, which, according to all spiritual teachings and inner paths, is none other than love. Love is the highest consciousness, the highest essence, and contains awareness, wisdom, connection, unity, offering, kindness, selflessness, respect, recognition, appreciation, gratitude, balance, serenity, bliss, purity. Everything that moves by love – from love, to love and through love – is positive, superior, right, or good. Anything else is inferior and, most likely, wrong, bad, or negative.

Fortunately, there is another very important detail: Karma as a whole, positive and negative, is at its core, in essence, all positive – positive and only positive. It is an opportunity to learn and grow, for each and every one of us. For example, you put your hand in the fire and get burned. You have a negative – unpleasant and painful – experience due to karma: the fire burns, and if you put your hand in it, you will burn. But through it, you learn and you do not repeat it. You gain knowledge and awareness, you are more conscious. You have grown, you have evolved. Karma leads to learning. Learning, development, evolution is the positive result, the positive essence of the law of karma, and this is done through everything, that is, through all the negative causes and all their negative effects – and not just the positive elements.

Through karma you become an alchemist of the spirit: just as alchemists tried to transform cheap metals into pure gold, so human beings transform the pain, the problems, and the difficulties into pure gold, through their life experiences: into knowledge of oneself, knowledge of others, knowledge of the world, life and the whole. Valuable lessons of the soul.

An economic collapse and misery in general in any country or part of the world are – on the one hand – the result of bad or negative karma. The people have not made their choices based on the highest energy and power, the highest possibility, love. They have not chosen anything with love – from love, for love, through love. If love seems a bit too sweet a word (you are probably confusing it or identifying it with romantic love) and you prefer a more pragmatic one, then replace it with another word, a concept that love contains: respect or appreciation, wisdom or awareness, unity or balance. The people have not chosen with respect, with appreciation, they have not chosen with wisdom, with awareness, they have not chosen with unity, with balance. Again, anything – a lot of qualities may constitute this choice.

On the other hand, economic misery and disaster in any country and part of the world are an opportunity to learn and evolve. They enable learning and growth, both for the whole and for each individual.

The "bad," the "dark," the "power of evil" on Earth, the elite, the few, the privileged, the – excessively and at the expense of others – rich, the powerful and the politicians, those in power in higher levels – it may seem that they are moving the threads and they are really doing it, but this is happening only on one level. On the external, material, earthly. On the visible and apparent.

Deeper, on a spiritual level, they provide the unfavorable conditions for the manifestation of the bad and unpleasant – for many – resulting from all the bad and wrong choices of the past. Without consciously knowing it, they are providing the negative conditions to manifest an unpleasant and difficult field, in which people need to fight, struggle and try, to learn, to grow and evolve into something else, into something better than it used to be, something better, both individually and collectively.

One may ask: "So, does this mean that we are to blame, the many, for the few having taken advantage of us, instead of the few having the responsibility, the moral and spiritual as well as the external and practical responsibility, of the evil that happens?"

No, it is not that the many are "to blame," by no means. The few have the ultimate responsibility for their choices and actions. And everyone pays for bad or wrong choices and actions, sooner or later, as karma has shown, so do not worry, because everyone reaps what he/she have sowed, what they deserve, at the end – or rather, along the way.

But the many have a responsibility to their lives and to themselves. Of their choices and actions in the "now." Haven't the previous "many," the previous generations made mistakes? Have they not accepted things they did not deserve (which no human being deserves)? Were they all infallible, perfect, driven by generosity, selflessness, and kindness? Did they have knowledge, awareness, were they aware of everything? If not, because the answer is "no," then the causes are shared there as well. Between bad or wrong choices of previous generations. We can take it even further and reach more metaphysical fields: that is, the wrong choices the people who live now made in their previous lives, create the situations they experience in the "now." Yes, this is also a possibility that one can take into serious consideration.

In order to understand better the issue of "fault" (or "non-fault"), as well as the fact that we take vital lessons from something, even though it is negative/unpleasant, we can examine this issue through something that is more direct and personal.

Let us take the example of the disease. Bad, wrong, negative choices can cause a disease. Is it the patient's fault? He/She may have made the wrong choices and the disease is the result of them, but the issue is not who is to blame or whether he/she is to blame! The "fault" becomes an issue, only in order for the person to discover the possible causes and cure them, to recognize them, and not to repeat them. When you say, "I'm to blame" for what is happening, it is not in order to belittle yourself but to take responsibility, to recognize the source, the cause, and thus to bring power to the present. To you completely and not outside of you, in the outside that is uncontrollable and "random."

You take responsibility and you take power and direction. But of course, you are not to blame, in the sense of accusation or criticism. You have contributed to the creation of something and by recognizing your contribution, you have the ability and the opportunity to reverse things, to change course, to recreate. Let's remove these words completely: "I am to blame," and "fault." After all, they have a negative sense and tone. Let's replace them with "I am responsible," "I have the responsibility," "I take responsibility."

A disease, although a negative, difficult, and unpleasant experience, offers a gift. The opportunity for someone to appreciate, to recognize, to fight, to turn. To learn, to grow, to evolve. Not everyone sees it that way and not everyone does it consciously, but we can use it for our own benefit, for the benefit of our soul. The disease gives the body the opportunity to manifest the negativity of many choices and the ability to that person to rediscover consciously, more deeply, as a whole, and truly, his/her health and strength. Many people, overcoming illnesses, feel fuller, more complete, richer, empirically and mentally, than before. They feel that they are living for the first time, that they are living for the first time truly, in essence, awakened. Consciously. Every moment counts and is important, sacred. They have more appreciation and gratitude for everything, two basic elements of true happiness.

The fact that situations – pleasant or unpleasant – are the result of karma, that is, the law of cause and effect, does not mean that we do not try to change things. The opposite! It means we have to try twice. An internal and an external battle. But it is a different battle. It is a battle against the evil self, individually and collectively. The negative self, the lower one, that moves from the ego alone and not from love and all that it contains. It is a call to discover how much power we have inside us, how much wisdom. To discover it and to practice it, to put it into action. To activate it and externalize it. A call to see how much love, how much light, how much goodness, offering, and selflessness we have within us.

This, above all: love. When you know the highest consciousness, the highest energy, the highest essence, the highest principle of all, love, then every choice, every action, every deed will be perfectly harmonized with it. And the flow will become good, positive, and pleasant again. Individually and socially, collectively, and personally. More and more good, positive, and pleasant.

It is in the hands of all of us, in the heart, mind, and spirit of all of us. Take on your part: recognize the law of karma everywhere, recognize the essence and value of lessons, take responsibility, thus bringing power back to you, move with love, from love, for love, through love and you will have contributed to the greatest extent, both in the evolution of your own self, and in the evolution of all.

SPACE ENERGY CLEANSING

How can I cleanse the energy of my house?

I feel the energy of a certain space to be somewhat heavy. Can I do something about that?

How can I cleanse the energy of a space where something bad or negative has happened?

How do I change the energy of the space in my workplace?

How do I make my home more positive energetically? To have good energy flow and harmony.

I moved to a new home/workplace. How can I cleanse it from old energies?

This is really such a popular and always relevant topic! Everyone wants to move and live in beautiful, clean spaces, which radiate harmony and positivity. There are many ways to cleanse energetically and charge positively our space. The following tips apply to any space: your home, work, and any other place you want to take care of, improve, elevate.

I. ESSENTIALS

* Cleanliness

First of all, something that is obvious but not always followed. Make sure your space is very clean, clean on the physical-material level and fully tidy. Dirt is negative energy – it cannot be stressed enough how much. The same goes for clutter. Clutter creates stagnant energy, while neatness and order create a harmonious flow. Try to clean your space with mild and as natural detergents if possible, which respect the environment. A clean, beautiful, tidy space symbolizes and mirrors a clean, beautiful, and tidy mind. When you clean and tidy what lies outside of yourself, the same thing happens on the inside. As outside, so inside, and as inside, so outside!

While your space should be clean and tidy, you do not need to be undue or obsessed about it. It is good to be able to enjoy the space, to live in it normally and not as if it were a museum. The obsession with cleanliness and microphobia create very bad energy conditions, while depriving you of all the joy and meaning. So, everything should be done consciously and in moderation, in a balanced way. We live, enjoy, and clean. We clean, enjoy, and live. Simple as that.

* Zen

After cleanliness, order, and neatness, it is very important that the space is "zen." Simple, minimal, without too many or any unnecessary things. Whatever you have not used in the last few years, free-cycle it to others who may need it and in this way offer more joy and positive energy. Alternatively, recycle it. It is very likely that you only need half or one third of what you have in your house! If you have the habit of collecting, keeping, stacking, storing, then reconsider. It does not benefit you and it is not good for you. On the contrary, it drowns you, weighs you down, limits you. A "zen," clean, minimal space, has the ability to be open, to accept, to receive everything new and good that the universe emits and which life probably sends you.

* Air and Sun

It is so important that the place is airy and sunny. Make sure that plenty of warm light enters your space and open all the windows, so that it is ventilated daily and, necessarily, every morning. No matter how much you cleanse the house energetically, if it is not relatively airy and sunny, it is a place that does not breathe and does not live. Sunlight and air are pure life and absolute positivity.

Avoid anything that dirties you or your space energetically. Negative thoughts and lower feelings, fear, sadness, anger, and everything else, as well as negative expressions, negative speech, quarrels, and tensions weaken, degrade, and disempower your energy. They soil you energetically, they create wounds or holes in your aura and drain you, or you just lose your vitality and strength. When these negative situations occur with great intensity and to a great degree and most of all repeatedly, they are imprinted in space as "negative energy." For your own good, and the good of all, of course, find ways to manage things differently. Choose more positive expressions and avoid as much as possible the intense and repetitive negative patterns, events and elements, in your space.

After – or in parallel with – these basic, necessary, and vital elements, that every space must have, we proceed to the very process of energy cleansing. There are a variety of techniques. Some are physical or material and some more inner or spiritual. They are all very easy and very simple. You can choose only one, a combination of them or even all of them! Experiment and apply the ones that inspire you and you like, for a perfect and really clean space.

II. NATURAL SOLUTIONS

We start with physical or material solutions.

* Salt

Let's start with my favorite method, so simple and easy and yet so beneficial and effective. You will feel your space completely clean. It is none other than water with salt. Salt, with its crystalline structure, is the most purifying element on Earth. It removes any kind of negativity, any negative or lower energy, frequency, and vibration. Use as little processed salt as possible, that is, use as much natural salt as possible (as, energetically, there is a difference between processed and unprocessed). Choose coarse sea salt without additives – you can find it easily.

Put two to three tablespoons of coarse sea salt in a clear glass bowl filled with clean water. Place the bowl of salt water in the center of the room and think about the intention, the reason why you are doing this: the energy cleansing of your space. For a more intensive and complete cleansing, place a bowl of water and salt in every corner of the room. You can use drinking glasses, preferably made of transparent glass (if possible, not colored). Do the same in any space you wish to cleanse. Leave them for 24 hours and then empty them, in the kitchen or bathroom, under running water (open the tap). The salt water has broken down or "absorbed" the negativity and has created a wonderful, clean atmosphere, sunny and sea-like! Repeat the process every now and then – for example, once every one or three months.

In a space where this is done for the first time or in a space that is negatively charged, follow this process daily for three days in a row or more, for example, seven days. Work intuitively; there is no rule in this. In addition, you can use salt in the water you use to clean the floor, as it freshens and energizes the space. It is really good; try it.

* Incense and Sage

Incense, as well as sage (the whole herb, not the tea!) are considered top elements for space cleansing. Their use has a long history and is part of many traditions around the world.

Light the incense and wave it all over the place as you walk around, staying longer in the corners. Let it burn. You can do the same with sage. Burn it carefully and wave it all over the place slowly, all around, a few times (intuitively, as much as you want; there is no rule). Many use scented sticks. Similarly, wave the smoke all over the space, walking slowly and meditatively around the room a few times, holding the stick close to the wall, staying longer in the corners. As you do any of the above methods, it is recommended that you have a clear intention of energy cleansing in your mind – that is, to keep this thought in your mind.

* Candle

The flame of the candle creates a truly wonderful atmosphere, warm and serene, an atmosphere that helps you focus inside. It purifies and illuminates energetically and spiritually. Choose white candles, which symbolize the spiritual light, the vital energy, the absolute positivity. The pure clarity and the clear purity! White includes and contains all the colors – that is, all the possibilities, the properties, and the qualities of life. You may also carefully place white tealight candles in the bowl with the saltwater of the first method, so that they float on the surface. If you wish to do an even more complete energy work, keep the intention of the energy purification in mind as you light the candles, dedicating them at the same time, to the higher wisdom and power. "I dedicate this candle to the highest wisdom and power. It cleanses my space energetically and fills it with light, vital energy, and absolute positivity. Thank you!"

Caution: always keep candles away from anything flammable, fabrics, curtains, etc. Never leave candles lit, unless you are in the room.

* Essential Oils

Essential oils, the super-super-concentrated power of nature, of flowers and herbs. The oils of flowers and herbs have an exquisite and truly essential aroma and a variety of beneficial properties: they relax, balance, help with concentration, bring uplift and euphoria. They should be completely natural and pure, not artificial or synthetic fragrances. Lavender, rose, sage, eucalyptus, tea tree, lemon, cedar, and juniper are some very popular essential oils for cleansing and refreshing the space. There are also ready mixes on the market. Let them warm in a special device that diffuses their celestial aroma. You can find such devices, as well as essential oils, in pharmacies and alternative stores or in stores with natural and organic products. You can also use them in the water you use to clean the floor. It is something that is often done by those who know their positive and beneficial effects.

There are also ready-made sprays with essential oils, such as the Aura-Soma® series. Spray well all over the space and corners. I have also been inspired and have created a series of energy sprays for space and personal energy, called Divine Life Elements!* You can look it up. But you can also make your own, by adding water in a spray bottle, and some drops of essential oils. Shake and spray.

Have a nice ethereal cleansing!

Caution: Strictly follow the instructions for essential oils. Essential oils are not drinkable and are extremely caustic. They are not used directly on the body (except lavender) but must first be dissolved in base oil (almond oil, for example). Keep them away from pets and children. They should also not be used during pregnancy.

* Crystals

Another amazing miracle of Mother Nature! Crystals are special pieces of the Earth, beautiful rocks, with unique energy characteristics. You can use crystals to refresh and elevate the frequency, the vibration of your space. To know their value and power, a few minutes of acquaintance with them is enough. Hold them in your hands and dedicate some of your time and attention to them, so that you realize what they are about! A large number of people swear by the beneficial and even healing properties of the crystals, and for good reason. They are wonderful in every way.

Clear quartz, the king of crystals! A crystal for all uses. A crystal that is clear light. It is light itself, in crystalline form. The etheric power, the vital energy crystallized in the kingdom of the Earth. Clear quartz always brings positivity and favorable flow in every space, influencing the energy, etheric, auric field. It protects and purifies, empowers and illuminates, rejuvenates and elevates. It is affordable, especially its small pebbles, and it is worth having some clear quartz in your space.

Clean and activate clear quartz crystals and place them around the space to create an energy grid, a field. For example, you can place one in every corner. You can use raw or processed crystals. Each form has its own value and beauty. Raw crystals are unprocessed rocks and look like pieces of broken stone or rock. They have primary and more authentic energy. The processed crystals are polished and cut into specific shapes, such as sphere, cube, pyramid, wand, obelisk etc. (they are also more expensive). They have the element of "sacred geometry," which is considered energetically and spiritually healing and invigorating.

In addition to clear quartz, very popular and important crystals are rose quartz and amethyst. Rose quartz is the stone of love. It inspires and transmits pure love, motherly love. Care, comfort, and warmth. Peace and beauty. Amethyst, with its wonderful purple-violet colors, is the stone of the spirit and offers spiritual protection and inspiration, spiritual connection, and guidance.

You will find crystals either in new-age stores or in specialized stores with crystals and stones. Visit them and choose your crystals intuitively. You can first consult a crystal therapy book in order to have a general approach and guidance, or you can ask for the help and advice of the people who work in such stores. But above all, listen to your intuition, your inner self. As you look and mainly, as you touch and hold various crystals, become more open and sensitive. Observe carefully: what are you impressed with? What do you like? What are you attracted to? Which one speaks to your heart?

After you buy and take the crystals home, cleanse them. Physically and energetically. Hold them under natural, cold running water and feel that they are rinsed both energetically and internally. Then, fill a bowl with coarse sea salt and place the crystals in the salt. Leave them for a few hours, not more than twelve. Rinse them again and leave them in the sunlight so that they are charged with vital energy. A few hours under the strong sunlight are enough. Then, take them in your hands and connect with them. Mentally, internally, energetically. Do a short meditation, while holding them in your palms, calmly and serenely. Take a few deep breaths and relax. As you hold them, bring the intention of activating them in your mind. With this intention, visualize a warm, bright, white light filling, illuminating, and activating your crystals. If you want, you can also talk to them, internally, spiritually, to express joy, love, appreciation, admiration.

The crystals are ready for use! Place them around the space, creating a crystalline field, an energy grid. You can place them in the corners of the space and one in the center, but also on the windowsills and at the entrance. Thank them mentally and feel the energy of the space being elevated, clean, and bright, as never before! Crystalline!

* Sound and Music

Special sounds and music have the ability to raise the vibration of the space and clean the "energy atmosphere." Many use bigger or smaller bells, singing bowls and gongs, or other religious instruments. You can find these in new-age stores. Music with sounds of nature (sea, running water, birds) and classical music are considered extremely beneficial and uplifting. Also, special relaxing music for meditation, reiki, yoga, massage, tai chi, etc. Spiritual music with prayers and mantras (sacred words of power), too. "Om" is the most famous mantra and is used by many. You may chant it out loud, repeatedly, emphasizing and holding first the "o" and then the "m" sound. Strong sounds can be equally effective, for example clapping your hands – however, you need to keep the intention of energy cleansing focused and clear in your mind.

* Feng Shui

We could not leave without mentioning feng shui – however, we will just mention it, not analyze it! It is a whole science of Chinese philosophy that relies on the five elements to create a good flow of "chi" (vital energy) in our space. There are many books one can buy in order to study and incorporate into their space some basic principles and tips. A complete study of the space by an expert in the art of feng shui is of course ideal.

Now, let's move on to some of the more esoteric, spiritual practices you can apply for an energetically clean, positive, and luminous space.

III. Spiritual Solutions

* Prayer

Prayer has great power. It radiates powerful positive vibrations and raises the energy of the one who prays but also of the space in which it is performed. Pray in the space you wish to cleanse, to charge positively, to illuminate, with this very intention. You can say the "Sunday Prayer," better known as "The Lord's Prayer." The energy of this sacred prayer is actually extremely high and powerful. You can choose another prayer that feels right to you. Say it out loud, as words have power and manifest what you say. Repeat it, three or more times, slowly and with faith. Try to mean and understand your words. Feel it. Do it from your heart and with all your being, become this prayer. Pray morning and night for three or more days in a row. In addition, you can ask a priest to perform a ceremony in your place and bless it. It is also known that spiritual icons create a clear and elevated spiritual atmosphere of constant protection and blessing.

* Meditation

One of the most evolutionary, healing, and beneficial types of meditation is called creative visualization. It is the ability to create mental images with our mind, usually in a state of deep relaxation, having a clear, focused, firm intention. Good, positive, ideal images, that we feel and experience as a reality, and energetically (etherically) they are indeed! This is a very effective method that renews and rejuvenates completely and instantly.

So mentally, with the power of your mind, fill your space with positive energy, with light. Light in – darkness out! First, take a few deep breaths to relax, ten deep breaths, slowly and steadily. Then, very calmly and serenely, imagine that light is filling your space. White light, clear, bright, white light. More specifically, imagine, as best you can, that clear, bright, white light comes from above, from the sky, and even higher than that, from a higher level of reality. Watch it descending and entering your space. Watch it radiating and swirling in the space. See or feel the white light spreading and intensifying, intensifying and spreading, becoming brighter and more luminous. White light fills the space completely and the space is completely filled with white light. Visualize it, with your mind's eye, and feel that it happens. Or simply, hold these thoughts constant in your mind, for a while. Take your time, do not rush, do it as calmly as you can. In a state of relaxation, receptivity. White light. White light everywhere. Clear. Pure. Bright. Radiant. Vital. White light is the absolute purity, the utmost positivity, life itself. The white light becomes even stronger, it cleanses and charges positively and vitally the whole space. It cleanses and removes anything lower and negative and brings only good. Everything good in life. Protection, peace, tranquility, harmony, beauty, flow, purity, health, abundance, power. As this is happening, feel more and more beautifully and brightly, more and more uplifted and euphoric. Finally, bring your attention to your body and take some deep breaths again. If you feel that you have "taken off," take some time to ground yourself. Drink water and take a shower. Sleep or rest. Or else, take a walk in nature.

Apply this visualization morning and night, three days or more in a row. The secret to success is repetition. If you want to create a highly positive and clean field in your space, once is not enough. Repeat and do it again; very soon, you will feel that it is working in a very positive way. And then, do it again!

* Invocation

It is similar to prayer – however, it also includes some positive affirmations, confirming and reinforcing an ideal situation. For example:

"Beloved, supreme and utmost love, wisdom and power of the universe and life, please cleanse, heal and fully illuminate my space. Please, remove anything negative and protect my space, absolutely and perfectly. Fill my space with light, positivity, with everything higher and good. With all the best. I affirm that my space is absolutely and perfectly clean and bright, 100% clean and bright, clean and bright on all levels. Let the highest good be done, and so it is! I am grateful, I am grateful for everything and from the bottom of my heart I thank you!"

As with prayer, do the invocation slowly, calmly, and meditatively, saying it out loud (this way, you reinforce the invocation with the power of speech), from your heart and with all your being, feeling and meaning what you say. Repeat it, three or more times, morning and night, for three or more days in a row. It works: do it and expect miracles and all the best!

* Reiki

In the second degree of reiki (the second level of training), we learn how to cleanse our space energetically. Energetically draw the symbol of power on every wall and hold it there for a while, mentally but also with your palms, giving life-force energy (reiki). Do it on every wall. Follow the complete method you have been taught in the seminar.

* Angelic Therapy

Do you know Archangel Michael? I do not mean personally! As an idea, as a concept. You probably know him, as he is the most known archangel. He who fights evil. He is the Power of God, the Will of God. In action, expressed and manifested, the protector of humanity. Not only in the Christian religion but in all three monotheistic ones – Christian, Jewish and Islamic. There are analogies in other traditions, as well as in Eastern religions. He is also the Archangel of Light, the ruler of the element of fire. He has the power to burn, to illuminate, to remove evil, to dissolve all negative energy, to cut all the negative cords, to purify on all levels. He is the great protector. As long as someone is open to him, and recognizes him. As long as one connects with him. Mentally and from your heart, from your soul. With your intention and faith, purely and sincerely.

Invoke Archangel Michael, call him, and ask him to clean the space from any negative energy and protect it. Ask for the presence of other supreme divine angels as well. Say it in your own words, simply, but with faith and will and from deep inside, from your heart and soul. With all your being. Say it several times, in the way you think is best. Do it morning and night, for three or more days, and see the energy of your space acquiring its most heavenly and angelic dimension!

"Beloved Archangel Michael, I invoke your Divine Power, Wisdom, and Love, your Divine Light, and I ask you to cleanse my space from any negative elements and to protect it absolutely and perfectly. Let the utmost divine angels of the utmost divine light fill my space with light, life, love, and everything beautiful, good, and true! With infinite love and infinite gratitude, thank you!"

Again, follow the rules and tips that apply to prayer, meditation, and invocation.

If you feel connected with, attracted to, or simply curious about Archangel Michael, you should dare to try it. Probably you will be amazed and pleasantly surprised. If you feel connected to him, if you have him in your mind and your heart, and you already feel appreciation, respect, and love for him, you already know what it is all about. Call him in your space!

At this point, the spiritual solutions for an energy cleansing of our space are completed.

I wish you to live, move, and always be in the cleanest, most positive, and bright space. In the most clear, positive, and luminous space possible.

MULTIDIMENSIONAL HEALING

Many Causes, Many Healings.

How many issues, difficulties, and problems do we have to solve... how many obstacles, how many blockages and challenges to face... in so many areas. Related to physical and emotional health, personal and family matters, love and relationships, loss and grief, responsibilities and obligations, work and finances, self-knowledge and self-worth, of existential and spiritual nature... Not only individually but also collectively, socially, globally.

If only it were easy... If only there were a cause for everything: a tangible, visible, unique, and specific cause. Where you could go and uproot it. Once and forever. So, easily and simply: uproot it, clean it... how nice would that be!

Georgios Mylonas (Geom!*)

Usually, there is more than one cause in every issue and situation, more than one cause for every difficulty, problem, and blockage in our multifaceted, complex, and turbulent human life. In our life here, on the – in other respects and in essence – exquisite, abundant, beautiful, and supremely wonderful planet, the planet Earth. There are many causes for everything. Everything that exists – everything that happens – is a result. A result for which there is more than one cause/creative principle. And then everything, every event, every result, becomes in turn the cause, which will be combined with other causes, in the creation of more results. And so on, constantly, forever... or as long as this world lasts!

There is more than one root in the tree of every event or situation and every situation or event is in turn the seed for something new. Seeds, roots, and trees. Trees, seeds, and roots, constantly. In the East, it is called the "law of karma," in the West the "relationship of cause and effect." In spirituality, we call it "divine/cosmic/universal justice," "life lessons," "spiritual evolution."

So, we observe that in everything, not only are there more than one operative-creative events, but also there are causes that are not visible – they are invisible to the naked eye, invisible to logic, invisible to the "now." They are intangible. Past.

According to trained and experienced holistic, energy, or spiritual healers, mystics, and teachers, there are many causes

172

for everything and in fact on many levels. Multidimensional. On levels beyond that of matter. Etheric and energetic levels, astral and emotional, mental and spiritual. Supreme and even higher. Immaterial, intangible, imperceptible, and even more subtle. Multidimensional.

Science, medicine, and psychology – like common observation and common sense – prove that we are creators and co-creators of our lives, responsible for our lives and our Being – if not partially, then completely.

Completely: at least in the way we act and react to existing external situations. We always have the freedom of choice, the freedom of choice of how we will act and react in every situation, in every event, positive and negative, good and bad, pleasant and unpleasant.

We also have the freedom and choice (although often not consciously) of how to perceive, how to filter, how to process, how to transform, how to assimilate, and, ultimately, how to use every event and situation for evolution – ours and everyone else's.

In addition, the modern sciences, medicine, psychology – and again, observation and logic – prove the relationship between soul and body, or more correctly, the effect of thoughts and especially emotions on the body, their effect on its matter and its health. Positive, superior, pure, optimistic, beautiful, bright thoughts improve health and strengthen the body, and all its systems and organs. The same and even more happens with the higher, clear, bright, happy, pleasant, peaceful, serene emotions. States of harmony, optimism, faith, love, and gratitude lead to increased health, but also to happiness.

On the other hand, negative, pessimistic thoughts and heavy, toxic emotions, with fear as a tyrannical king and anxiety, sadness, bitterness, jealousy, envy, guilt and anger as miserable royal subjects, will burden our health and lead, with mathematical accuracy, to misery.

It is a fact that none of us is born with the talent or the predisposition to think and feel good, beautiful, and positive, everywhere and always, in all situations, every moment! Or... is this how we are born... and in the process something... "breaks down?" Whatever happens, focused positive thinking, optimism, conscious choice and the frequent experience of positive emotions and expressions are – to a large extent – an acquired process. We learn, we are trained, we are initiated to think and empathize from a higher level of perception, clearly and brightly, harmoniously and healthily.

Spiritually. Truly. Essentially. Authentically. Independently. Freely. Lovingly. Compassionately. Unitedly. Peacefully. Consciously.

We slowly make it a habit, a way of life, feeling, thinking, perceiving, from the heavenly level of the Higher Self, of our spirit and soul, of our true Being.

We learn it and make a conscious effort, every day, every moment, in more and more situations, in more circumstances, problems, and issues that concern us personally and the whole in general. Consciously, we make an effort and we consciously try. With an open spirit and an open mind, we learn to open our hearts and hands, our bodies, we learn to observe, hear, see, feel, appreciate, and care for them. And we try to relax, to empty, to let go, to allow healing and health into our Being.

We place our intention, we focus, we realize and discover that effort often requires "non-effort," the opposite of effort, the opposite of action. But it takes a lot of effort to reach the awareness of non-effort; of letting go, relaxing, harmonizing, releasing, loosening up, emptying and refilling, stopping, resting, allowing, accepting, listening, feeling, observing, learning. For most, non-effort often takes effort... is that a paradox? It is similar to the human nature: Spirit and soul in the world, in matter, unlimited and perfect and eternal in the limited and imperfect and finite.

And although science and psychology – and also, as we have said, both common sense and common observation – demonstrate the importance of thoughts and emotions, of consciousness itself to body and matter, to health and disease, the great healers, teachers, and mystics take us even further and reveal more hidden, invisible worlds, worlds of causes for everything that happens. More causes for a disease. Or for an issue, for a situation.

Emotional and mental causes, energy, and etheric causes. And higher or deeper, spiritual causes: karmic reasons, actions, and thoughts we did in another life. Before we were born, on other levels and dimensions. And the phrase "You reap what you sow" returns for the – pleasant or unpleasant – reaping of our "then" good and bad seeds. Karma? Cause and effect? A forgotten cause, lost in time, in the records that only our soul and God know – and maybe the angels?

Karma? Or possibility, opportunity, a call for change? For transition, ascent, evolution? The cheap metal of negativity and darkness becomes the gold of higher perception and light. From weakness to strength, from pain to love, from ignorance and amnesia to awareness and wisdom, from non-consciousness to consciousness. From ego to Being. From the war of matter to the peace of spirit.

Yes, karma, but not as unjust criticism, revenge, punishment. On the contrary, karma as something we deserve in order to rise, to learn, to become better. To be enlightened and enlighten. Our existence, the world, and everyone. Karma is not a punisher, it is not an enemy. It is a friend, it is an ally, a supreme teacher, and a great guide. Always on our side, always for our good. It is the way to everything good, the Divine way, the way to the Divine.

We are constantly learning through the Universal Teacher of Evolution, the spiritual and material law that governs and exists in everything and anything. We learn through Karma: whatever you sow, you will reap, and you reap what you have sown. We learn through the cause-effect relationship: everything has a cause and everything is a cause for something else. We learn – sooner or later, easily or stiffly, pleasantly or unpleasantly – and gradually evolve through negative and positive experiences of our past, our childhood, our birth (even pregnancy) but also the time before our birth.

Do we have past lives? Yes, it is possible, if not certain! But it does not matter if we believe in them or if we know them. Through karmic lessons and the cause-effect relationship, through the Gift of our Consciousness, a truly supreme Divine gift, we gradually learn to eliminate negative behaviors and adopt positive ones. To overcome selfishness and to adopt kindness, generosity, and selflessness. To go beyond the lower emotions – not by suppressing them, but by expressing them as well, as we are human beings, after all. But now we do not stay there, not so often, and not so much. We learn to experience more and more often more joy and peace, love and compassion.

We become better, brighter, lighter, more "spiritual" (dare we say "more divine?") and more human. With karma as our ally, friend, companion, teacher, and guide – and so much more – with our past as our guide and ally, as the valuable record of experiences, negative and positive, we train and move ourselves toward our evolution, toward our ascent to Self-Knowledge and Self-Realization. Toward Enlightenment and Theosis, following the example of great teachers. And fortunately, they were the greatest in the history of the planet, leaving their golden writings, their golden examples. Their words are still burning, fiery, in heaven and on Earth.

It is clear that the past leads to the present, to the "now," to the moment, to what I am, what you are, and what we are. But hold on… what I am, we are, and you are is not only the result of the past, it is not only the peak of the iceberg of experiences, the peak of the iceberg of karma. We are not just a whole. We are not just a result. We are also exceedance, transcendence. We are spirit and soul, invisible and intangible, though in the visible, in matter. In this world, but not of this world. We are transcendental soul and spirit, and our consciousness is the sign but also the proof, the tool, the means, the bridge.

So, although we are the result of millions of causes, known and unknown, visible and invisible, past and even more distant, emotional and mental, spiritual and karmic, we are something more: infinitesimal and at the same time infinitely maximum: we are transcendence, consciousness, spirit, and soul. I am transcendence, consciousness, spirit, and soul. You are transcendence, consciousness, spirit, and soul. We can always realize this: we can become even more our spirit, and soul. The strong, the powerful, the pure, the bright. The eternal, one with the Divine Principle, the Source of All.

We can become more of our spirit and soul, consciously, here on Earth, in the "now," in the "here and now." Become because we are *not*? No. Become what WE ARE and become BECAUSE we are, because THAT is what we are. Is this a paradox? Yes! It is similar to human nature: precious gold behind cheap metal, spirit behind matter.

Enough with the philosophies — as beautiful and useful and enlightening as they are! Let us return to the issue we started with. An issue has many causes: known and visible but also invisible and unknown, on many levels, from unpleasant or pleasant emotions and negative or positive thoughts to spiritual and karmic causes.

Similarly, a health problem, like any blockage, difficulty, or challenge we face in our lives, contains more than one cause. Something that occurs in the body has many possible causes:

Biological causes: Causes in the cells and chemistry of the body, in malfunctions of organs and systems. In the genetic code. Hereditary.

Environmental causes: Toxins from the environment and unnatural lifestyle. Pollution. Bad nutrition. Sedentary life. Anxiety.

Energy causes, energy disharmony: The chakras, the energy centers of the energy-etheric body malfunction. They are not developed, they are closed, sluggish, dirty, or blocked. They are in imbalance. They need cleansing, healing, charging, activation, balancing. The aura, the outer shield of the energy-etheric body, is weak, dirty. It may have holes, tears, leaks. It needs empowering, charging, cleansing, strengthening, restoration.

Causes in the psyche, the emotional field, and the field of the mind: The emotional and mental levels/bodies are blocked. There are many or strong negative thoughts and toxic or repressed emotions such as fear, sadness, anger. Consciously or subconsciously, present or past. We need to recognize them, to accept them, to process them, to release them. There are also ways, standards, and patterns of thinking, negativity and pessimism that are burdensome to health. There is no flow, no confidence, no hope, no joy. We need to focus on higher and more positive situations. This focus should become a habit, our second (or first) nature, a daily practice.

Spiritual causes: There are spiritual, karmic causes, something we have to clean from the past, something that "chases" us. The soul demands balance, justification, fulfillment, evolution, assimilation, progress, the soul demands self-knowledge and self-improvement. Do we need something to learn, to recognize, to see, to hear, to feel, to accept, to understand, to realize? Yes! What is this? What does our body tell us? What does our instinct, our intuition, our logic tell us? Our feelings? Our soul? What does our life tell us? Do we listen? Do we see? Do we feel? Do we recognize? Do we accept? Do we understand? Do we realize? Do we learn? Slowly or fast? By force, painfully, unpleasantly? Or with intelligence, with joy, pleasantly?

There are many causes and we need to know that they exist, although the knowledge of what they are exactly is often not direct. The physical, self-healing powers, and innate abilities to heal and balance our body, mind, and psyche, spirit, and consciousness are infinite and unlimited, perfect and complete. Amazing and exquisite and an inconceivable miracle, but 100% true and real. However, in order to activate them, you often need help, external help. The external environment, changes, new ways of thinking, of expression and behavior, new habits and patterns, re-adaptation, modification, improvement, refinement, and additional changes.

There are many elements "out there" that help "in here." And many other souls who help "this soul here." They want to help and it does them good. As you want to help and it does you good. To offer, to participate. To communicate, to collaborate, to exchange, to accompany, and to be in step with. One of the most difficult parts of any healing, on any level and in any field, is its beginning: recognizing the need for external assistance and requesting it. Going there and bringing it to us.

There are many elements, tools, and aids and many people who can support and participate in identifying, releasing, and treating causes. Causes of all kinds and levels. An energy/holistic therapist can help significantly in healing and strengthening the energy-etheric body, chakras, and aura. Reiki is an excellent method for this, like all energy therapies.

A mental health counselor or psychologist will greatly assist in recognizing and processing emotions and thoughts, understanding, adjusting, or releasing them. In identifying and processing ways of action and reaction, patterns and standards of expression and behavior. It may help us to see ourselves better. Recognition, acceptance, understanding, forgiveness, freeing, and release are important keys to mental healing, healing on an emotional and mental level.

To overcome any difficulty, problem, blockage, or disease, it is necessary to make many changes, changes in consciousness. In thought and emotion. It is imperative that we learn, train ourselves to see, to perceive, to express ourselves positively, to think positively, and to feel even better. Positive statements, books, and seminars on self-help, self-awareness, and energy techniques are ideal. As well as visualization, daily relaxation – total and deep relaxation – and meditation.

Laughter and joy are real medicines. Instant, effective, elixirs! However, we speak about the abundant laughter, the ripple, and the spontaneous joy. The pure, the innocent, the childlike, the unlimited.

Taking responsibility for ourselves, our lives and our health is a big (huge) step and it means that we're becoming more "adult." At the same time, it means and includes that we're becoming more childlike. Pure, innocent, happy, free. Without weights and other unnecessary things. The adult does not leave behind the child (the childhood, the child self, the innocence, the creative curiosity, and the pure joy), but he/she encloses it. He/she includes. He/she contains it. With love, as a precious and sacred part of his/her Being, of the past and of the "now," because he/she really is. Who can grow old or be unhappy if they have – they are – an inner child?

As we have said, meditation, visualization, positive affirmations, and self-help books and seminars, as well as energy and holistic techniques, help in the positive change:

they strengthen the energy, the aura, and the chakras; they release negative emotions and patterns and motivate us to focus to the good and useful. They lead to overcoming karmic lessons and obtaining the necessary and valuable – for our development –knowledge from them.

But beyond the mental-emotional and energetic changes, other changes are also necessary: changes in matter. Perhaps you need more movement. Walking, running, swimming, dancing, gymnastics, yoga. Sedentary-static-immovable life is stagnant, self-destructive, and sick because it is not life. Life is flow, it is motion, and flow and motion is life.

Probably you need "more nature." Frequent walks/hikes in nature, rest and rejuvenation in the forest, on the beach, in the mountains. More breathing: deeper, bigger, more substantial, more conscious, more vital. Again, in nature, in a clean environment, in a clean atmosphere. Frequent, conscious, slow, deep, vital, enjoyable breaths. In the green, in the forest, in the mountain, at the sea.

Perhaps you need more water. The sacred essence of life and vitality. Or a better diet. Whatever Mother Nature produces, as natural and pure as possible – fruits, vegetables, nuts, fresh and colorful – and away from anything artificial and fake. It is known even in the most remote and isolated part of the world (or rather, especially there!) that herbs are the pharmacy of nature. There are herbs for everything and a vast bibliography of information and research on them. In addition, the so-called "superfoods" offer essential elements, protection, and energy in a difficult, artificial, and unnatural environment and lifestyle that drains the human daily.

You might need better sleep, more rest, more pause and relaxation. Away from stressful environments, people expressing negativity through their behavior and thinking, away from images and sounds of ugliness or violence. Or you may need more care and love – not maybe; for sure! Human contact, touch, hugs, caresses, kisses, companionship, company, friendship, family ties, communication, all without exception are infinitely and absolutely important.

Speaking of touch, care, and contact, the technique and art of massage is perhaps the most underrated healing process in the modern Western world. In reality, however, massage is a complete as well as a deep care of the whole body. But not only that – it is a deep and complete care of our psyche. It completely relaxes and rejuvenates. It balances, harmonizes, and strengthens our whole being. It restores us. On all levels. Aromatherapy massage, Swedish massage, Thai massage, reflexology, shiatsu, and ayurvedic massage (and so many more) are all excellent techniques, with countless holistic therapeutic benefits.

Energy techniques such as reiki, pranic healing, crystal therapy and aromatherapy, acupuncture etc., have a very important effect on psychosomatic well-being. There are a variety of other energy techniques, such as quantum touch, theta healing, body mirror system, spiritual response therapy (SRT), emotional freedom technique (EFT), family constellation, that help unblock many levels of our Being and contribute to a more holistic approach. In addition, homeopathy and Chinese medicine are gaining trust and are the choice of more and more people.

As we proceed with the healing of our Being, another element is considered of utmost importance: Faith. Probably (or rather, for sure!) we need to strengthen our relationship with the Higher, no matter how we approach, perceive, and understand it – or do not understand it (why should we understand it anyway?). However we call it, no matter how we refer to it, it does not "misunderstand" us, at least not as an ordinary person would. We cultivate and strengthen our relationship with the Higher through prayer, meditation, fasting, service, study, and faith.

And we finally come to medicine, where every effort to heal the body and the human psyche usually begins. Science has made amazing leaps in treating all the health issues that concern man. It offers immediate relief and, very often, immediate and easy healing. It is important not to see all sciences as enemies but as friends and allies and in no way to underestimate their achievements. They are important achievements throughout the lives of countless people who have been devoted and dedicated to this sacred purpose.

Just as we use countless technological advances to make our lives easier and more comfortable, so we use medical procedures (examinations, medications, surgeries, etc.) to address complex and multileveled issues that concern us.

People who live more consciously, more spiritually, more naturally and more completely, more thoughtfully and emotionally, who perceive things more substantially and farther, know the benefits and gifts of medicine and use them whenever needed, always according to the advice and guidance of specialists. But unlike the mass of non-thinking, non-emotional "others," who operate mechanically and often robotically, they approach each issue in a deeper and more holistic way. More substantially, more spiritually, and more consciously.

In short, they choose the changes I have mentioned. On every level. They choose learning, improvement, self-knowledge, evolution. They do all the steps. With the often miraculous, modern medical methods, combined with a holistic, conscious, energetic, emotional, mental, and spiritual approach and healing, health, strength, well-being, and harmony return more steadily, more deeply, more substantially, and more truly on all levels. And with them, they bring the energies of happiness, fullness, and bliss.

Again, enough with the philosophies and prompts, no matter how helpful. Let's move on to something direct and practical in the "now," right now!

ENERGY TECHNIQUE OF
MULTIDIMENSIONAL HEALING

Sit comfortably, with your back straight.

Take three deep breaths. Slowly, calmly, deeply, down to the abdomen. Inhale, slowly and steadily through the nose, exhale, blowing slowly and steadily through the mouth.

Place your hands in prayer position, joined in front of the chest.

Again, take three deep breaths.

Then relax, let go, allow yourself to relax more and more.

Imagine you are sitting under pure energy, a shower of positivity, a shower of White Light. Pure, bright, White Light, absolute and perfect positivity, life, and love.

Imagine it, see it mentally, and feel it. Or just assume something like that is happening. Raise your awareness, open up, become more receptive.

The White Light showers and surrounds you. The White Light penetrates you and fills you. The White Light illuminates you completely, fully, to every point, completely, everywhere, White Light.

Again, take three deep breaths and feel that you are filled with the clear, bright, White Light.

Think that the issue that concerns you is solved, cured, on more than one level. On many levels. On every level. Imagine it, see and feel the positive emotions.

Take three deep breaths, as your issue is resolved and healed completely and perfectly, on all levels.

Say the following positive affirmation (open your eyes and read it). Repeat it three times. Slowly, consciously, mentally, or out loud. Meaning and feeling what you say.

"Perfect and Complete Healing on All Levels!

Perfect and Complete Multidimensional Healing!

Energy of Life, Vital Light!

I send Energy of Life and Vital Light to my issue. I release and heal the causes on all levels.

Energy of Life, Vital Light!

I release and heal all the causes in my body, the ether, my psyche, my mind, and my spirit.

Energy of Life, Vital Light!

I replace fear, all negative emotions, and negative thoughts with acceptance and love.

Energy of Life, Vital Light!

I create and experience joy, health, harmony, balance, purity, serenity, freedom, fullness, wisdom, strength, awareness, consciousness, enlightenment, on all levels.

I am grateful and I thank you, Energy of Life and Vital Light!"

Stay in it for a while and feel the energy or anything else.

Finally, take three deep breaths again and open your eyes.

Repeat daily, or whenever you need it.

Know that you deserve the best, the best possible life, that starts from today, that starts with every breath, that starts from now, from this moment. You are soul and spirit beyond any problem, issue, and situation, any disease and cause and effect, beyond anything material and beyond this world. The journey of consciousness, of spiritual and total self-knowledge, of perpetual evolution, of enlightenment, and finally of theosis, is what is worth more than anything, above all.

And you do not just deserve the best, the best possible life – you deserve what is worth more than anything, the journey of consciousness, all that you live. But you are not worth only this, because you are spirit and soul, so you are already a value in itself. You have worth and you are a value; value absolutely has worth – independently, everywhere, and always. Value has worth by definition, from essence, from its reality.

Perform good work – pleasant and enjoyable, because success is certain – in everything you do, in everything we do, always with consciousness and love. Highest and absolute consciousness, absolute and supreme love!

BLISS: THE 24 GOLDEN STEPS

※

If happiness had secrets, what would they be? If it had steps?

Study these 24 secrets, the 24 golden steps. They will lead you where you want to go... to your bliss!

Are you ready? Let's go, let's start. The 24 golden steps of happiness and bliss are offered generously to you. They invite you and spread out in front of you, open and bright...

1. THINK LIKE A PHILOSOPHER!

First, most basic, and supreme: Know yourself. Or, at least try! Who are you? What are you? Are you your body, your experiences, your memories, your personality, your strengths and abilities, your flaws, and your challenges? Are you something more? Yes, you are your potential as well. You are something bigger than what you appear to be, something bigger than what you express and what you see or believe you are. You have countless possibilities. You are a small and, at the same time, a great miracle of nature, of life, an unexplored and wonderful miracle. One can say that you are a divine work, a supreme divine work, and in fact of the supreme divine art!

Open your eyes and mind, to the unknown, wonderful, bigger You, that is open to your hidden possibilities. To your hidden wisdom and power. Recognize yourself in a new field, in a new range, in a bigger, higher, and deeper field and range, and then your life will take a new breath.

Remember: You are an open field. You are what you choose to become. You choose what you are.

2. CREATE AS A CREATOR!

You are not a victim. You are not a weak being. You are not an animal (although they are so admirable and lovable), nor a plant (although they are so beautiful and wonderful), nor an object (although they are so useful and valuable)! You are a strong, intelligent, spiritual being. You are a creator.

Create, co-create, together, in collaboration, with the forces of life, nature, and the universe, a better "today" and a better "tomorrow," for you and for everyone. You can do it and it is the best thing you can do. Everything else is just an aimless, pointless waste of time! So get out of the mentality of the victim and the weak, shake it off immediately and completely and realize the great creative power, the great co-creative power that you actually have.

3. ACT LIKE LOVE!

Do what you love.
Discover new things you love to do.
Do what you do, with love.

These are three different acts of love. Read them again.

4. LOVE AS YOURSELF!

After the "know yourself" (or before it, or in parallel with it), comes the equally well-known "love yourself." Do not be afraid – it is not about narcissism, nor about egocentrism, egopathy, or egoism. It is something deeply essential and extremely vital, it is really healing, a healing of yourself.

Love yourself truly, deeply, completely, just as you are now, with all your faults and flaws, with all the wounds of the past. This is the closest, the most valuable that you have. Love yourself as if you were your child. So truly, so deeply, so completely. "Embrace" and accept your "child," yourself, you, completely. Without "if," "should," and "when."

Love is the supreme wisdom and the supreme power, the supreme consciousness and the supreme energy. Love is light, love is life, and love heals, not only mentally but also physically. It heals existentially, completely, it heals on all levels. If you water with love, with the wisdom and power of love, the consciousness and the energy of love, if you water with it every cell, every molecule, every thought, memory, and action, can you imagine how it will be, can you think about what will happen?

You will have changed, you will have been transformed from within. You will have become what you always wanted to be, even if you could not express it in words: yourself, you, in its most beloved, cured, and complete version.

5. FEAR, OUT!

Release the fear. This is something that cannot be stressed enough! It is your "enemy" – I exaggerate, in fact we have no enemies, but if we had, it would be one for sure! Fear limits and deprives us of every joy. It is an artificial, non-natural limit that you set for yourself and does not serve your life and evolution. We always talk about unnecessary, meaningless, and pointless fear, the fear without any obvious cause of danger. Fear easily turns into anger, sadness, and any other negative emotion. Anger, sadness, and any other negative emotion contain fear. In their roots. It doesn't do anything good to you! Decide and choose to transcend your fear. Decide, choose, and live, as your spirit: without fear, freely, peacefully, ecstatically, and completely.

6. BECOME TALENTED!

Discover your talents. You have countless! Unleash your creativity. You have infinite! What would you like to do? Something you would like to try? Discover the arts and creation, the arts and creation of all kinds and all forms, and then your life will never be gloomy, dull, or colorless again.

7. NIGHT AND DAY!

Love sleep, and also love movement. Appreciate action and non-action. Every night, rest deeply, rest completely, rest truly, every night. Just before you go to sleep, take some slow and deep breaths, and mentally release, simply with the intention, whatever weighs you down, whatever thoughts and feelings, the past and the future. Let go, in complete trust and real enjoyment, in the peaceful embrace of sleep, of divine sleep. Allow it to make you a brand new being, until the morning, after it uplifts you sweetly to heavenly dreams and heavenly places!

Simultaneously, and in parallel with sleep and rest, love action, love movement. You know it is good for the body and offers you health, don't you? Exercise, gymnastics, walking, running, sports, dance, martial arts, yoga – there are definitely many types of movement and training that not only will you like, but you will love. Add daily movement in your life and everything, really everything, will move with you and will move better.

8. THE FOOD OF THE GREAT MOM!

Be aware of your diet. You are what you eat. Or, rather, you are – also – what you eat! Focus on what nature creates and offers, whatever comes from Mother Nature. Fragrant, colorful, delicious, juicy, crunchy vegetables, fruits, and nuts. Anything that is simple, natural, and unprocessed by man. They are the cleanest and highest energy food you can have. Make all of these a big part of your diet, if not the biggest. You will rediscover your true "taste" and you will feel full of energy, vitality, and strength. Eat consciously, eat naturally.

9. A DIFFERENT FAMILY!

Animals and plants are the best companions! Love them, take care of them, put them in your life, and they will offer you an ocean of pure love and joy.

10. DO NOT BE RESTRICTED!

Stop caring about the opinion of others and behaving accordingly, trying to be liked. They judge only one side of you, an aspect, completely superficially, and according to their own beliefs, their own mental and emotional structures, and all the other filters of their mind and self. They do not know who you are. They do not know who they are. Even you do not know who you are! Every day you are something more, every day you are something new, every day you are more of yourself.

Free yourself completely from the judgments and criticisms of others. If they are not true – and they are not, because, as we have said, they are subjective views of a temporary or past side of you – it does not concern you. And if it does not concern you, it does not hurt you. Live for yourself, make sure you are true, be yourself, and – although you will not do it for this reason – others, sooner or later, will appreciate it much more than anything else.

11. DO NOT RESTRICT!

Stop judging others. How they live or what they should do. Everyone has the right to do what their soul desires to do and everyone does what they know – to the extent they know. Stop all criticism – it is a waste of time and energy. With criticism, you often enter a vicious cycle of conflict and not of substantial improvement, so if you realize that something like this is happening, make sure you get out of that cycle immediately. Stop criticism or mitigate it or postpone it, until you know more about that situation. Do not jump to conclusions and do not move without thinking. And of course, strictly forbid to yourself any gossip and any kind of evil-based humor. It is difficult for some, but it is necessary.

If you decide to criticize, do it with great respect and love, without selfish motives. Without a deeper need to appear and prove "right" or "good," or superior in some way to the one you judge. If you judge, judge after a lot of thought and introspection about your motives. Follow the golden rule: do not do to others what you would not want others to do to you. What is it like to be the other person? What is it like to be in the situation he/she is in and how could he/she be helped? Speak with respect and love and give others complete freedom. The beauty of life is its huge variety: every person is unique and adds something different on the canvas of this world. Liberate and empower others, liberate and empower them in every way, if you want life to do the same for you.

If you see something that you think is wrong, you will clearly say it, you will express it. After you have processed it well and filtered it, first. You will do it with respect and love – out of love and respect. Always keep in mind that the highest judge is life, existence, the Absolute/the Highest/ the Divine. Avoid polarization and extremes, and practice circular views, spherical views, multifaceted views, total-holistic perception, and handling. Do not reject, do not separate; connect and compose. Adopt other perspectives and prisms, so that you gain insight and understanding of issues and situations.

Dedicate the energy you have for criticism (yes, man has such a great mood and a lot of energy for it) to you, and dedicate it to what you like to do. To something essential, creative. Dedicate your energy and time to your work. By creating the life you want and experiencing higher levels of bliss and completeness, you give others the example and the stimulus to do the same.

12. RELATE WITH FREEDOM AND COMPLETENESS!

Connect yourself, relate yourself, communicate more genuinely with others. When you are yourself, without pretense and without masks, when you are honest, authentic, and simple, you create the strongest and most wonderful relationships you can imagine. Conscious, beloved, supportive, evolutionary, full of meaning and substance. When you are full of love, interest, and care for another, when you have absolute respect and deep appreciation for

Esoteric Answers

another, when you function from a point of freedom and completeness.

This is one of the greatest secrets of relationships, of all relationships: to be and to function – to think, to feel, to act – from a point of freedom and completeness.

"I am free, you are free. I do not bind, I do not deprive, I do not control, I do not oppress, I do not restrict. I am complete, you are complete. I do not beg, I do not steal, I do not depend, I do not drain. Together, free, full, and complete, we consciously move, by choice, into a relationship of love, communication, respect, and joy."

To understand it even better, imagine the relationships created by non-free people who feel empty, or "half." Sooner or later, there will be a disaster! But now imagine the relationships that free, full, and complete individuals create. From the beginning, true perfection! Move toward it – it exists, and yes, it is possible! Those who experience good personal relationships belong to this second category. If you move in that direction, realizing what is best for you, you will be tuned in to those people who are in the same flow.

13. MEDITATE LIKE A YOGI!

Discover the power of meditation. Ten to twenty minutes a day, with your eyes closed, in complete relaxation, just observing your breathing, will bring amazing results. You will be renewed mentally and emotionally, spiritually, and energetically, even physically. There are many additional types of meditation, such as gradual relaxation, creative visualization, candle gazing, repetition of mantras (energy words of power), and dynamic, dance, or walking meditations. Read related books, search related videos and instructions online, go to groups and seminars, and experiment a lot. By experiencing the power of meditation, its wisdom, harmony, and serenity, you discover the power that exists within you, your wisdom, harmony, and serenity.

14. PRAY WITH YOUR SOUL!

Discover the power of prayer. Connect with the Divine element. Yes, the higher element exists and yes, you can do it, you can connect more with it. More than before, more than ever. Prayer will change your life. As much as only a connection to the higher/the divine can.

15. SPEAK LIKE AN ANGEL!

Practice focusing positively. Choose carefully what you say and how you say it and speak with love and encouragement, with respect and appreciation, both to yourself and to others.

16. SAY WHAT YOU WANT!

Discover the power of the Word. Speak consciously and speak positively, so that you direct the energy where you would like it to go. Confirm mentally – but also with your words – health, vitality, love, romance, friendship, abundance, prosperity, good work, inspiration, creativity, joy, peace, fulfillment, enlightenment, and all the best! Speak consciously and positively and in this way, direct the energy consciously and positively. Make it your second nature, or even better, first.

17. A GOOD DETOX!

Do a detox from negativity. Make a list of anything you consider negative: difficult people, negative environments, processed foods, fats, meat, sugar, salt, flour, cigarettes, television, negative thoughts, stress, anxiety, anger. Reduce them or eliminate them for a while – or for longer – from your life. Start with three days and then make it seven, if you can. Real, total, deep detoxification. You will feel great.

18. CLEAN OUTSIDE, CLEAN INSIDE!

Clean and tidy your house. Clean it on an energy level as well. You will feel like you are cleaning and tidying up your inside, yourself, but also your life.

19. VITAL PAUSES!

Add more relaxing moments to your daily routine. Close your eyes and take ten deep breaths, slowly and steadily. Inhale through the nose, slowly down to the abdomen, then exhale, blowing slowly through the mouth. Then just let go and relax, even for a while. If you cannot do it, just imagine what it would be like if you relaxed, if you relaxed completely! Or say, "Tranquility, tranquility on all levels," several times, slowly and calmly, and then surrender to it. Take these breaks often and whenever you need them.

20. GOOD MORNING, I APPRECIATE YOU; GOOD NIGHT, I AM GRATEFUL TO YOU!

Start and finish your day with appreciation and gratitude. Declare that today will be a new, beautiful, magical day, and finish your day at night by thanking it for everything it gave and taught you.

21. HOLY HANDS!

Find ways to offer. To another, to all others. Even a single good deed or a nice word counts, has value, and contributes. Offer as much and to the extent that you yourself would like to be offered.

22. ONE WITH NATURE!

Visit nature. It is your mother and your true home. Hug, touch, talk to the trees. Talk to the sea, to the sky, to the sun, to the stars. Connect, open, feel, relax, breathe. Rest and rejuvenate, deeply and completely. Feel unlimited joy and gratitude for the gift of life. Do it at every opportunity.

23. ADD LOVE!

Put love in everything. Love is the sacred, the miraculous, the highest element. The magic, beauty, and alchemy of life. It heals, transforms, changes every negative situation into something higher. It brings light everywhere and always. Love, love, and love to all, love, love, and love in everything.

24. THE CHILD IS THE KEY!

Make the big comeback: become a child again! Discover your lost – essentially, your repressed – childhood. Children hold the key to the kingdom of heaven and the secrets of life as well.

Observe: What is it like to be a child? What is a child like?

A child expresses itself freely and genuinely, authentically and truly. It expresses all the emotions, it expresses them directly, with intensity, completely. It is absolutely in the "now," in the moment. There is neither yesterday nor tomorrow. Only "here," only "now." It is itself, just itself, without a second thought, without masks and roles, without pretense. Nevertheless, it plays, plays, and only plays. Life is an open field for play, discovery, experimentation, and exploration. Everything is unknown, magical, new. It explores, experiments, discovers, learns – rediscovers and learns constantly. Nothing is the same, to be taken as it was given, or gloomy. Everything is wonderful!

Observe the children – they are great teachers – and become like them. Do not be afraid and do not worry: You do not lose what you have learned, what you have gained, you do not lose your adult self. You do not lose your strength and responsibility, or your maturity. You just rediscover that part which will give your responsibility and maturity, your knowledge and experience, your adult self, the one element they lack, what they need more than anything else. The element that is absolutely important, absolutely vital for them to continue. This element is joy. The joy of the game, the joy of the unknown, the joy of learning. The joy of simplicity, the joy of exploration, the joy of miracles.

So make a big comeback: become a child again and allow the joy to come back, to come back again and fill your life!

LOVE

The most perfect element,
The primary light,
The brightest energy,
The most beautiful word,
The sweetest feeling,
The purest thought,
The highest act,
The maximum value,
The deepest knowledge,
The innermost power,
The most sacred teaching,
The most vital learning,
The most blessed purpose,
The existential peak,
The clear starting point,
The selfless intention,
The first need,
The most ardent desire,

Georgios Mylonas (Geom!)*

The most luminous vision,

The unlimited joy,

The incomparable bliss,

The eternal peace,

The initial religion,

The final science,

The secret art,

The supreme philosophy,

The essential self-knowledge,

The continuous expansion,

The constant elevation,

The most beneficial development,

The most positive evolution,

The most ecstatic transcendence,

The infinite happiness,

The oceanic fullness,

The heavenly freedom,

The inconceivable reality,

The inseparable unity,

The total enlightenment,

The absolute perfection,

The real cure,

The best decision,

The rightest direction,

The ultimate solution,

The true answer,

The ideal destination,

The most open road,
The most enjoyable route,
The only option.

LOVE.

Did you enjoy this book?

Giving it a review would be greatly appreciated!

Made in the USA
Las Vegas, NV
27 February 2024

86345181R00122